*Islam feels like it must defend Allah and even to do his killing, abusing and terrorizing in the name of religion. I believe this eye-opening work will save many from falling into this trap unaware and be used to set others free who have been deceived. The world is waiting for the truth and needs to hear this truth now!*

—REV. DR. VICTOR N. MANASSA
SENIOR PASTOR, FIRST ASSEMBLY OF GOD
BRADENTON, FLORIDA

*This is interesting and informative reading! Through persecutions, fear and distress, W. L. Cati gives firsthand insight into the truth about Islam and the hardships this religion places on women married to Muslims. May the Lord use the truths in this book to break the strongholds of Islam and bring freedom, honor and respect back to women, as God intended for them to enjoy.*

—NICHOLAS A. MANASSA
ASSOCIATE PASTOR, FIRST ASSEMBLY OF GOD
BRADENTON, FLORIDA

# MARRIED TO MUHAMMED

W. L. CATI

**CREATION**
**HOUSE**
**PRESS**

MARRIED TO MUHAMMED by W. L. Cati
Published by Creation House Press
A part of Strang Communications Company
600 Rinehart Road
Lake Mary, Florida 32746
www.creationhouse.com

Unless otherwise noted, all Scripture quotations are from the Holy Bible, New International Version. Copyright © 1973, 1978, 1984, International Bible Society. Used by permission.

All Scripture quotations marked KJV are from the King James Version of the Bible.

All Scripture quotations marked AMP are from the Amplified Bible. Old Testament copyright © 1965, 1987 by the Zondervan Corporation. The Amplified New Testament copyright © 1954, 1958, 1987 by the Lockman Foundation. Used by permission.

All Scripture quotations marked NKJV are from the New King James Version of the Bible. Copyright © 1979, 1980, 1982 by Thomas Nelson, Inc., publishers. Used by permission.

Quotations from the *Qur'an* are from *Yusuf Ali Qur'an Translation and Commentary, Pickthall Qur'an Translation, Qur'an Transliteration Maududi Surah Introductions, Qur'an Subjects, Yusuf Ali Qur'an Subjects.*

Library of Congress Catalog Card Number: 20-01093484
International Standard Book Number: 0-88419-794-8

01 02 03 04     8 7 6 5 4 3 2 1
*Printed in the United States of America*

# ACKNOWLEDGMENTS

A special thanks goes to all those who prayed W. L. Cati through and back to the cross.

To her parents, Johnnie and Charles, for all their love, to a mother that kept believing the Lord and faithfully having others pray with her: Thank you for never giving up.

Thank you to all who believed in W. L. Cati, supported her dreams and visions, and held up her arms when she was weary.

A deep heartfelt thanks and love to her husband, John. Thank you so much for your patience, love, support, prayers and faith, and for truly being her Abraham.

Thank you to Sharen, Kay, Linda, to all her children and grandbabies, and to all the pastors who supported her.

Special thanks to Sharen for her hard work, and to John for the hours of editing, praying, loving and supporting.

Most of all, thank You to Jesus, for loving W.L. Cati when she was still a sinner and for taking what was intended to be evil and making it all good.

May all of you and all the readers of this book be blessed according to the prayer of Jabez:

> Oh, that You would bless me indeed, and enlarge my territory, that your hand would be with me, and that You would keep me from evil, that I may not cause pain!
>
> — I CHRONICLES 4:10, NKJV

# DEDICATION

This book is dedicated to my family,
children and friends, and to my
husband, John.
Love to all of you!

To all who cannot yet glimpse the
Master's plan for their lives:

**THROUGH HEAVEN'S EYES**
by Stephen Schwartz

A single thread in a tapestry—
Though its color brightly shine—
Can never see its purpose
In the pattern of the grand design.

# TABLE OF CONTENTS

## Part 3

# INTRODUCTION

Zennah Ministries, Inc. would like to thank everyone for making this book possible. We hope it will help others from falling into the trap of Islam.

A word of caution: What you are about to read may shock you. The Hadith's and Surah's quoted in this book are narratives from Islamic sources. We have quoted many parts of this book from Islamic Web bases, not Christian sources. Anything that is in **Bold** and *Italic* is cut and pasted from an Islamic source.

Zennah Ministries, Inc. was established to help the many women who are bound under Islam. Our mission is to reach out to women everywhere, helping them learn to stand firm in their faith in the Lord Jesus Christ, to heal and to overcome all of the various types of abuse they have suffered.

Zennah Ministries, Inc. is an information base for anyone who would like to know more about the uprising of the Muslim religion. Women all over the world are marrying Muslim men, thereby increasing the number of Muslims in astounding proportions. In fact, this trend is one of the leading factors contributing to the fact that the Muslim religion is the fastest growing religion in the world.

Zennah Ministries, Inc. feels that the body of Christ needs a wake-up call. We believe that Christians must be informed about the Muslims and their Islamic aspirations and plans for the future.

Our dream is to one day provide places of refuge by opening houses where women can feel safe and take time to heal. We are striving to open these safe houses because the need is so great and there is little assistance currently available that helps rebuild the lives of these abused women and get them on their feet again.

Zennah Ministries, Inc. has done extensive research and has firsthand Islamic experience. We can provide the real truth about the deception regarding Allah, the Qur'an, Mohammed and the Last Days.

Visit our website at:

## www.zennahministries.org

Father, the time has come. Glorify your Son, that your Son may glorify you. For you granted him authority over all people that he might give eternal life to all those you have given him. Now this is eternal life: that they may know you, the only true God, and Jesus Christ, whom you have sent. I have brought you glory on earth by completing the work you gave me to do. And now, Father, glorify me in your presence with the glory I had with you before the world began.

—JOHN 17:1-5

# CINDERELLA'S TEARS

*lyrics written by Deborah R. Struder*

There was a time when I thought my Father God had
    left me behind and all alone I was given to the
    wicked stepmother's world.
Desperately trying to make a family from my enemies.
And finding myself a slave to what had become of me.
I forgot where I came from.
I forgot whose name I wore.
I forgot who gave life to me.
I'd forgotten my very royalty!

Cinderella's tears I've cried
Cinderella's fears I've felt before
And I've known the pain of lost inheritance
Your Father cries, yes, your Daddy weeps for the love
    you don't see.

You believe for others but think he won't do the same
    for you.
Desperately trying to win God's approval and failing
    miserably.
Won't you open His love letter and let Him open your
    eyes to see.
To see where you came from.
To see whose name you wear.
To see who gave life to you!
To remember your very royalty!

MARRIED TO
MUHAMMED
MARRIED TO
MUHAMMED
MARRIED TO

# PART I

# TESTIMONY OF W. L. CATI

## *FROM BEAUTY QUEEN TO THE VEIL OF ISLAM, FROM ISLAM TO JESUS!*

I think I always deeply believed in God. I can remember that when I was as young as four years old, I would always cry whenever a conversation about God came up around the dinner table.

Even though I was raised in a Christian household, no one in my family really went to church or prayed—other than on Easter Sunday or Christmas. I had a good family; there were no drugs, alcohol or abuse. My father, grandfather and uncles worked hard five to six days a week to provide for us, and they were always home on time.

As a teenager, I started down the wrong road. But when I was seventeen I began going to church on a regular basis. It was my mother who first got me to go. She never said a word about participating in church activities; but when she began to attend regularly, I saw such a change in her in such a short period of time that I had to go just to see what it was all about. Then in one small moment of time, as I knelt down at an altar, Jesus changed my whole direction and purpose in life.

Within a year's time, my whole family started going to church. I told everyone about God: my classmates, my teachers and even strangers. I saw many people follow in my footsteps. I wanted everyone to know about God and what God meant to me. I served the Lord for many years. I even had a singing ministry and had won several beauty pageant titles, one of which was Mrs. Alabama—I placed in the top ten in the Mrs. America pageant. I traveled all over the U. S., but then as my fame started to grow, I started taking my eyes off the Lord and putting them on how wonderful I thought I was.

My life up until that point had been somewhat sheltered. I was just experiencing the nightlife for the first time. That's when I really started to stray from my religion. It was during this time that I met Muhammed. I met him in a nightclub. I was there with my aunt, who had just lost her husband of twenty-five years to cancer, and I had just gone through a divorce. We were at the bar to drown our sorrows. I had only been divorced for six weeks and certainly was not ready to start any kind of a relationship with a new man. I was just there at the bar to have a good time and to maybe dance off a pound or two.

A lot of men asked me to dance, but I wasn't interested. Apparently, Muhammed had been watching me from across the bar. I later learned that his wife had just left him that day. He walked over to me and asked "What if a nice guy asked you to dance? Would you?" There was something about him that I liked, and for some reason, I agreed to dance with him. And he sure knew how to dance! He twirled me, spun me, threw me and, literally, swept me off my feet! For me, it was love at first sight. This was my first real encounter with a worldly man. He was so exciting. We talked all night about many different things; but somehow we managed to avoid the subject of religion. At first, he gave me a bogus name, but later that night he finally told me his real name and where he was from. I didn't know much about his country; and therefore, I didn't ask any questions about it. I only knew it was somewhere near Egypt. From that day on, we were together almost every day. We had our ups and downs, and our break ups, and I knew he was seeing others. But because he hadn't said the "I love you" stuff yet, I didn't think I could hold him to any type of commitment to me. So, somehow, we always got back together.

My parents were very concerned. They knew I had lost my faith, but they still had hopes that I would return to Jesus. They didn't approve of our relationship, and we had many battles. It eventually got to the point where I hardly spoke to my parents. Of course, I thought I was old enough to make my own choices without any input from them! Plus, Muhammed didn't get along with my mother, so I had to make a choice: Muhammed or my mother. Actually, He really didn't like any of my friends or anyone who had supported or loved me in the past. Gradually, my old relationships grew fewer and fewer, until my only friends were his Arabic friends.

Muhammed and I continued to date on and off for almost a year. Then on New Year's Eve, he asked me to marry him. I was so happy, even though I knew it wouldn't be an easy life together. I recognized that we had been raised completely differently, we had come from two different areas of the world, our religions were different and even our reactions were different.

But I loved him so much that I couldn't stand to be away from him. I even experienced what seemed like physical pain inside when we were apart. He had become my whole life. I felt so secure when I was with him. My every thought centered on him, and I trusted everything he said. He was so handsome with his dark hair, dark eyes, strong build and olive complexion. Plus, because of the way he could con everyone, I thought he was so very smart.

I spent hours imagining what our children would look like. When he asked me to marry him, I said "yes," and we decided to be married exactly one year from the date when we had first met. He told me that for our marriage to be meaningful to him, he wanted to be married and raise our children in his religion. He said he believed his previous marriages had failed because he married outside of his religion. I loved him so much that I agreed with anything he asked. I didn't realize the impact of my words until much later. He took me to the mosque to become engaged, and called his family in Syria to tell them the news.

On March 30, 1986, exactly one year and a day after we had met, we were married in the mosque. I did not know about his religion, and at that time I did not concern myself with it. The way he explained it made it sound so much like my own Christian beliefs. He told me *Allah* meant "God" in Arabic. He said that Muslims believe in Jesus, heaven, hell, the Ten Commandments, angels, the prophets and the Bible. It wasn't until much later that I found out the truth about just how different the two religions really are and the life-threatening mistake I had made.

The ceremony in the mosque was very different than a Christian wedding ceremony. Muhammed was on one side of the room and I was on the other side. A curtain physically divided the women from the men. I was asked to repeat many things in Arabic. I did not have anyone there with me—no friends or family; nor did I have anyone there to translate what was being said. The women would just nudge me, and motion for me to say "yes." After the wedding, I was given a cookie. I took a bite, and then my husband was given the rest. It seemed like hours before I saw him again. No kisses were exchanged. In fact, he was very cold with me. When we got into the car I tried to read the marriage licenses. I soon discovered that my name (and my religion!) had been changed. When I started to get upset about it, Muhammed told me to not to worry because it was only on paper. He smoothed things over by saying he knew that I had not changed in my heart.

While I was expecting our first child, my husband took me to my first "Deedat" debate, via satellite. Deedat was a great debater for the Muslims against the Christians. He was very convincing, and since I hadn't been practicing my beliefs for sometime now, I listened to his every word. That's when the doubts took over. I was suddenly full of questions, so I started asking every Muslim I knew to tell me about Islam. I also read all kinds of books on the Muslim religion.

To honor my husband's wishes, after our daughter was born I took on the responsibility of being a teacher of his religion. My husband did not practice his religion, and I felt the need for the children to know something about God. Although I wasn't practicing Christianity, I took the children to church on Sundays and to the mosque on Fridays. I went to Arabic school and Muslim school. I started reading books on the life of Muhammed and on the lives of all his wives. I also watched all of Deedat's videotapes. I tried to read the Koran, but couldn't make much sense of it. What made reading the Koran so difficult was that I had to perform all these washing ceremonies to read it, and be completely covered in order to even touch it. At the time, that was too much bother for me, so I took my husband's and other people's word for it. Over the next six years I was torn between the two religions—my husband's and mine.

Before long, we had two beautiful children—a five-year-old daughter and a two-year-old son. Muhammed and I were fighting a lot. He was staying out all night several times a week and the physical abuse had really heightened, along with the emotional, verbal and sexual abuse. I was becoming desperate for my marriage to work. I had failed once before and didn't want that to happen again. I was to the point of trying anything to make him love me.

He sent me to Syria, and there I converted to Islam. I started covering, (covering is a part of life for Islamic women), praying five times a day and fasting. Every year during Ramadan, I would go to the Mosque to pray. I read books on how to be a good Muslim. I just knew this would make him love me, but it didn't. In fact, now he and his mother threatened me even more. Now that they had me, the truth of the religion started coming out. The main thing I was told was that if I converted back to Christianity I could be killed, and they would tell me stories to prove their point.

Deep inside, something was missing. I didn't feel complete somehow. I had no joy inside, and no real peace in my life. It seemed like something was always going wrong at home. Family arguments were constant. I had suffered all kinds of abuse from my husband and from some of his family members. I also knew that my husband was cheating on me—I just couldn't prove it.

Every time the family would get together, they always ended up fighting, yelling, fussing and screaming over little things. At times, dishes would fly, food would fly, and one time, my husband's mother actually threw hot water on him and he grabbed her by the neck. My husband's temper was so bad that if someone just pulled out in front of him in traffic, he would chase the person down, and pull out his gun so the person could see it. He broke doors and made holes in walls with his head or fist when he would lose his temper. He always kept some type of firearms with him. Our home was full of all kinds of weapons. I often worried that someone was going to get killed. There was never peace. Dinner time in our house was a nightmare; nothing was ever good enough I was always walking on eggshells. On many occasions I would have to leave the table because I couldn't stand it.

Aside from all of this, trips together with his family were impossible; there was always a big blow up over the smallest thing. During one trip we took across the country with our children, mother-in-law and brother-in-law and his wife and child, the fighting began the moment we started out. Halfway through the trip, it got so bad that we ended up leaving my husband's brother, wife and child and went on without them. Where was God's peace, love and joy? It most certainly wasn't in my life or my household.

Before long, my husband and I had four children: a daughter, a son and a set of twins (a boy and a girl). My mother-in-law had come for a visit; and my husband, who was her oldest son, took on the responsibility of caring for his mother. I always got along with her in the past, but this trip was different. She began trying to take over my household, and we started arguing often. She didn't like the way I did things nor did I like the way she pushed me around. She would even go through all of my personal things! It got to the point where the tension was so great, and I was so angry, that we didn't even speak to each other.

By the time the Christmas holidays came, things were well out of control. Muhammed and I had completed building our new house in Florida, and the children and I were the only ones living in it. My husband was still living part-time in our home in Georgia, traveling back and forth from Georgia to Florida, running the business in both states. We had over fifteen stores between both states, and the money was flowing.

He had come to join the kids and me for the holidays when I noticed he looked extremely tired. Originally, we had planned to be in Florida full-time by then, but it wasn't working out that way. We decided that the children and I would move back to Georgia until all of us could be in Florida together. We closed up our new house for a while and headed for Georgia.

We had only been back in Georgia for a month when a neighbor from Florida called. She was a friend, and a real estate agent. She wanted to know if we would like to rent our house to a ladies' group. "Sure," I said, anything for money. Little did I know who these ladies were.

My mother, a wonderful Christian lady, had been living in Florida for almost twelve years, and had attended a women's Bible study for over nine years. My parents had rarely talked to me about my change of religion. Instead, they just loved me and silently prayed. Every year, without fail and without my knowledge, my mother would write a prayer request asking the ladies to pray for my family and me. She told them all about how I had converted to Islam and was covering up with the veil.

In March, this group of ladies started coming into my

home for one weekend each month. During their meeting they saw a picture of my mother and me. They also saw all of the Arabic things in my home, including the mosque we had built downstairs. (It even had a clock that chimed whenever it was time to pray). It did not take them long to put it all together and realize mine was the family in need of prayer. They prayed all over my house. They prayed in every room, over every picture, over every thing. They prayed that I would come back to Jesus.

In June, I returned for a visit. I had been going through all kinds of turmoil in Georgia. I was still fighting with my mother-in-law, and I was very upset over the many things she had done. I was also becoming extremely confused about religion. After I returned to my home in Florida, I felt God was really speaking to my heart. (I did not know those women had prayed over everything in my house). Out of desperation, I called a neighbor who lived down the street from me. I had heard she was a very devoted Christian woman, so I left a message on her answering machine saying that I wanted to talk to her about God. However, she was out of town for the summer and did not receive my call.

This time the children and I stayed in Florida for about a month. Then I called my husband in Georgia and told him that I just didn't want to live in Georgia anymore. I told him that I loved Florida and was happy there.

He said it was fine with him, but I would have to come back to Georgia to move again. So, at the end of July I went back to pack. Back in Georgia, my battle continued with my mother-in-law. However, when I told her of my confusion about religion, she suggested I pray and then God would show me.

That was exactly what I had been doing, and did He ever show me! She also said something very profound.

She said my problem was that I worshiped my husband, and my husband worshiped money. Boy, did that hit a nerve or two. She was right: I was worshiping my husband and his religion. That's when I realized I had forsaken Jesus for a man.

While Muhammed was helping me pack up the car as we were getting ready for me and the children to leave for Florida, I noticed something that concerned me. I looked closely at him because he was holding his chest and breathing very hard. He was also very sweaty. When I asked him if he was OK, he said he was just tired.

The children and I drove late into the night before we reached Florida. We got in so late that I decided to wait and call my husband after I got a little sleep. After my nap I immediately went to work putting things away. I was so busy that it was already 10 P.M. when I realized that my husband still hadn't called me. I tried calling him, but no one answered. I called his car phone. No answer. I concluded that he had probably gone out to eat somewhere, and I would talk to him later.

Early the next morning I tried to call him again. I called the house first, no answer. The car phone, no answer. I called all the different stores; but no one had heard from him. This was so unlike him. So I waited another hour and made another round of calls. Still no one knew where he was. I finally broke down and called his brother. I really had a bad feeling by now. I didn't know what might have happened, but I felt something just wasn't right. A deep, sinking feeling came over me and I began pacing around the house. After several hours, the phone finally rang. It was my husband, but he sounded strange. I asked him where he was, and told him that I had been trying to reach him since the night before. I'll never forget his words.

He said, "I'm in the hospital. I had a heart attack yesterday." My first response was, "You're kidding me?" I couldn't believe it! I knew something was wrong, but a heart attack? He was only thirty-six years old. How could that be possible?

He told me he was fine and that he would be getting out of the hospital the following day. I tried my best to stay calm for his sake, and for the children, who were now standing around me. I asked him how he could be fine. I didn't understand why the doctors would let him out of the hospital the next day. Because he sounded so very weak and disoriented, I asked him what I should do. He told me he was fine and that I should do nothing. I asked him for the doctor's phone number, but he wouldn't give it to me. I persisted until a nurse finally got on the phone, talked with me and gave me the number.

I was in tears when I called the doctor. He came to the phone immediately and told me that my husband was very sick. He said my husband had suffered a severe heart attack and I needed to get back to Georgia as soon as possible because no one else could sign papers giving permission for Muhammed to have the necessary surgery. The doctor also told me that Muhammed was on morphine, which explained his stupor.

When I hung up the phone, I fell apart. I tried to tell my children; and then I called my mother, but she could barely understand me. I knew I had to calm down because panicking was not going to help matters any. I had to make some decisions and fast. Would I fly or drive? Take the children? I decided to call my dad and he helped organize the trip. My mother was to come along and help me with the driving. We packed very quickly and we were on the road in less than an hour.

Immediately after we arrived in Georgia, I dropped

my mother and children off at the house and headed for the hospital. I got to Muhammed's room in the intensive care unit at about 3:30 A.M. Here was my big and strong husband, now lying there so weak, so helpless and so tired. He looked up at me and smiled.

He tried to reassure me that he was fine. I don't think he really knew what had happened, or how serious it was. He kept telling me he was going to get out of the hospital the next day. He was on drugs and delirious. I could only stay with him a few minutes at a time. The nurse came in and told me where I could sleep. I didn't want to leave him, but she insisted that I rest. Evidently, she could tell I was very tired, so she convinced me to go down the hall to a waiting room where the chairs converted into little beds. I tried my best to sleep so I could regain my strength. Only God knew what was ahead.

The next day we learned some of what had caused the heart attack. A blood clot had closed up 98 percent of an artery. If the blood thinner could not dissolve it, Muhammed was facing surgery. The doctor kept him on medication for three days—with no success.

When I went to the house to pick up the children and my mother-in-law to bring them to the hospital, I explained to them how sick Muhammed was. I also specifically told my mother-in-law not to take any cigarettes with her into the hospital. I explained to her that this was very necessary because the doctors believed Muhammed's cigarette smoking might have caused his heart attack. I stressed the fact that he was on heavy medication, and that he might search her for cigarettes. I begged her not to give any to him.

Our visit went great. Then as we were getting ready to leave, Muhammed insisted on walking us down the hall. He started asking his mother for cigarettes. We all shouted, "NO!" But he grabbed her purse and started looking for one. Then right there in front of the children and me, my mother-in-law reached in her bra, pulled out a cigarette and handed it to him. We all screamed at her. My husband promised he wouldn't smoke it.

I had never been so angry with any one person in my whole life as I was with my mother-in-law at that moment. I simply couldn't hold it in. I demanded, "Who will take care of all of us if your son dies?" Her cool response was "if God wants him to die, it is God's will." I told her to leave it to God then, He didn't need her help.

The next morning I arrived at the hospital very early. When I walked into the room, I smelled smoke. Yes, it was a non-smoking room (with oxygen); but I smelled smoke. I looked at him and said, "Where's the cigarette?" He told me that he had only smoked two puffs, but when I searched the room I couldn't find the rest of the cigarette. I then left the room to go get a cup of coffee and to talk to the nurse. She came back to his room with me to try to talk some sense into him, and to get him ready for the heart catheterization.

On our way downstairs for him to have some tests, I looked at his face and saw that his eyes were glossy, his skin was turning ashy and his forehead was sweaty and clammy. He was having another heart attack! This couldn't be happening! It hadn't even been thirty minutes since he had smoked that cigarette. I was extremely upset. However, the doctors reassured me that he would be fine.

He came through the test and soon he was back in his room. I again tried to get the rest of the cigarette from him, but couldn't. I stayed with him all day; and then later that evening, I went downstairs for a few minutes to grab some dinner and bring it back to the room.

When I came back a short time later, Muhammed was standing by the window: smoking! I ran into the room, grabbed the cigarette out of his hand and flushed it down the toilet.

I knew his mother, brother and uncle were on their way to the hospital. I had not told them about what had happened that morning. I was trying to just let it go. I got him back into the bed and started to eat my dinner. But just minutes later, that dreadful look came over him again. I called the nurse, and she came running in. Immediately, the medical team sent me out of the room. Doctors and nurses were all running here and there, coming and going from my husband's room, wheeling in all kinds of medical machines. I became hysterical as I watched all of this urgent hustle and bustle going on while I, helplessly, stood by in the hall. Nurses surrounded me and tried to settle me down; but when my husband's mother, brother and uncle walked up, I jumped my mother-in-law!

My husband's family immediately started taking sides. His uncle sided with me, and my husband's brother took sides with his mother. The immediate medical crisis did pass, and the day finally came for my husband to come home from the hospital. However, another huge fight broke out, and that same night Muhammed had to be rushed back to the hospital by ambulance. Tensions were so great that my heart cried out, "When will it all stop!" Muhammed wanted to leave Georgia and go back to Florida as soon as he was able. He was very upset with his family for many reasons, and he wanted to get away from them as soon as he could.

As soon as he was able to travel, I made a bed in the back of the car for him to lie down on during the long ten-hour trip back to Florida. Then as we were driving away, my mother-in-law yelled at me, telling me I was trying to kill her son.

I had received my answer from God. This was not a religion I wanted to be any part of. There was so much hate, malice and confusion all the time. And I knew my God did not have these attributes.

After we had been back in Florida for about a week, the neighbor I had called at the beginning of summer returned my call. We didn't talk too much because my husband was around, but we met for lunch and I told her all of my problems. She invited me to church; and the next Sunday night, my children and I went to the service. My husband had said it was fine with him since I was a Muslim. He even told me to go if it made me feel better. "Just do not ever change your religion," he said. I really had no intention of changing it because I thought maybe I could be both, maybe go to church and still remain Muslim. I thought I might be able to believe in the good things of both religions.

That night my feet weren't even in the door of the church when I started crying. I couldn't stop the tears from flowing freely. My children kept asking me what was wrong, I tried to assure them that I was fine. I can't remember what was said during the sermon that night, but God was talking to my heart. During the service the words to an old song I had sung years ago kept playing over and over in my mind, "Jesus is the Cornerstone." I knew that was my answer: He, Jesus, was the answer!

A few days later I picked up the Bible to read it and the pages fell open to this passage: "That their hearts might be comforted, being knit together in love and unto all riches of the full assurance of understanding to the acknowledgment of the mystery of God, and of the Father, and of Christ; in whom are hid all the treasures of wisdom and knowledge. And this I say, lest any man should beguile you with enticing words. For though I am absent in the flesh, yet am I with you in the spirit, joying and beholding your order and the steadfastness of your faith in Christ" (Col. 2:2–5).

I found my way back to the Lord Jesus and my children followed right along with me. Of course, this decision enraged my husband. One night at the dinner table he told me that he was giving me two weeks to come back to Islam or he was going to throw me into the streets. That night, with my children sitting there, I looked at him and said, "I am ready to die for Christ, and He will take care of me." Then my husband said to me three times, "I divorce you!"

The next day the children and I moved out to our small house. It has not been easy. There were many threats from Muhammed and his family. The children and I were spit on, hit and cast out; but we believed the Lord would continue to take care of us. The peace we had in our new home and in our hearts was worth giving up all the other. And there were many material things to give up!

I tried many times to win Muhammed and his family over to the Lord. This went on for over a year. I had hopes he would come to Jesus. Muhammed actually went to church with us a couple of times. He even went to my first concert where the Spirit of the Lord was so strong that our youngest daughter gave her heart to the Lord. Each time my husband and I would talk about the Lord, I could see the Lord dealing with his heart; but then soon afterwards he would become harder and harder to Jesus. I even took his mother to see Billy Graham. Instead of her being touched, she insisted that all the people at the crusade were lost. She also said that Islam could use speakers like Billy

Graham because he was such a great communicator.

The final act was the night I washed Muhammed's feet with oil, water and my tears. He was moved to tears, but later that night I found him in front of a pornography site he had pulled up on the computer. I went upstairs to my prayer closet and cried my heart out to the Lord. The Lord spoke to my heart and said, "Hate even the clothes defiled by the flesh." I didn't know that verse and even questioned it. But it was like I could see where his clothes had been. I could feel his clothes speaking out to me, telling me stories of places they had been and all they had seen. Then the Lord revealed to me husband's plans. His plans were to acquire everything and leave the children and me homeless. I felt the strong need to get out of that house quickly and retreat to our small house that was only a few streets away. Muhammed had taken all the equity out of our other homes, and was now planning to move to the small house himself. His plot was to take the equity out of the small house and leave me with no way to support our children and without any place to live. This was his strategy to keep us dependent on him so that he could maintain control over us. As I was lying on the floor in prayer that night, I saw it all so clearly.

The next morning I found those verses in the Bible that the Lord had used to reveal to me what was taking place behind my back: "Be merciful to those who doubt; snatch others from the ire and save them; to others show mercy, mixed with fear—hating even the clothing stained by corrupted flesh," (Jude vv:22-23).

When I then asked the Lord if I had I forgiven Muhammed, I felt the Lord speaking: "Yes, seven times seventy." I began to count all the nights when Muhammed went out over the fourteen years of our marriage, remembering that he had gone out at least twice each week! (Two times 52 times 14; that was 1,456, much more than 490). The very next night was the night that Muhammed gave me the command to either come back to Islam or be thrown into the streets! In spite of it all, God's grace has been sufficient to help me to forgive. Yes, every day I forgive him and his family because just like those to whom Jesus was referring when He said, "Father, forgive them, they know not what they are doing" (Luke 23:34), Muhammed also had no clue! Now I pray blessing on him and his family. The Word of God says to bless those who curse you (Matt. 5:44). I still believe God for his salvation and for the salvation of many other Muslims. My children and I pray that Muhammed and his family will come to Christ. We know that Jesus loves and died for all of them, just as He did for us.

Since we took that bold step of faith and made the decision to serve the Lord and not man or false religion, my children and I have seen many miracles in our lives. For over a year we lived totally by faith, without any formal forms of income coming into the household. We know for a fact, and from experience, that God can take what was intended for bad and make it good. During that season of our lives my new quote became "Jesus can take our leftovers and make goulash out of it, and feed the world."

Indeed, there has been a price to pay, but I thank the Lord Jesus for paying the ultimate price for me, the price for my salvation.

The Lord has been so faithful to us, over and over again proving Himself, His love, His grace and His mercy. Out of all this pain, a ministry was birthed. The Lord has blessed us with a wonderful ministry where we are seeing many come to Christ and are able to help other women who are in the same situation we were in. At Zennah Ministries, Inc., we have a deep burden for the lost Muslims and for the many women and children who suffer great abuse at the hand of Islam.

Many have asked me, "How do you get a ministry started?" My reply is simple and to the point: "You don't!" The night I left, and as I was going through everything, I never once said to myself, *Wow, this could be a ministry.* All I did was become very burdened for the lost, the Muslims and hurting women. I just started sharing my story with others—one on one—in hopes that maybe my life could help someone else.

One night when I was praying and feeling so bad about leaving the Lord after I had met Muhammed, the Lord really spoke to my heart. He said to me, "Cati, when you left Me, you had a small singing ministry started; but now you have a real burden for the lost souls. You truly know how lost the lost are. You have a burden for the abused woman; you know their pain." Those were the sweetest words to my ears. His sweet words set me free, and this ministry was birthed—not for my glory, but for His Glory! It is all about hurting people: It is all about Jesus!

I want to add this statement: In no way do I (or others in our ministry) believe that all Muslims beat their wives. Abuse from anyone is very wrong. It comes from everywhere, from all types of people, in all walks of life. The difference, however, is that in Islam, men are given permission to beat their wives...with no questions asked. Please pray for us as we continue to reach out, as the Lord leads and guides us, to those who are hurting! We need your support, time and prayer. It is a big call, and I have made the choice to answer it. Will you help? It is not by our might, but by His! Please ask the Lord to show you how you can help us. The harvest is ripe!

## FINAL NOTE FROM W. L. CATI

Many times Muslims and other people have asked me why I came back to Christianity. Many have made the assumption that it was my Muslim husband's fault because he did not treat me well. However, they have been wrong when they have jumped to the conclusion that I changed my religion because of the actions of a man. However, I want to make something very clear: If I based my decisions on people, whether they were Christians, Muslims or Jews, I wouldn't be anything. NO one is perfect, except the Lord of course! We have *all* sinned and fallen short of the glory of God!

Instead of looking at the people around me, I compared the lives of Jesus and Muhammed. It was Jesus, whose life was so different from anyone else's on the face of this earth, that led me back to Him. It was His perfect life, His love for me and the whole world. It was how He gave up heaven, came to this world and died for us; It was how He took on our sins so we could all have a relationship with God! This wonderful Jesus is what drew me back to His precious side, back to my home in Him.

And no, I do not follow Jesus because of the fear of hell or the promise of heaven. I choose to follow Jesus because He loves you and me so much. Jesus never killed anyone, but instead He healed the sick and brokenhearted. He lived a life of perfection and can forgive all of our bad deeds.

On the other hand, what did Muhammed do? Well, we know he led many battles, looted, forced others to follow him, had many wives and even took a small child to be his wife.

Can Muhammed offer God's forgiveness of your sins? No!

Does following Muhammed ensure you of the promise of spending eternity with God in heaven? No!

Is Muhammed dead or is he alive? He is dead!

My friend, Jesus is alive and well. He is working on your behalf, seated right next to God Almighty. And He is coming back very soon!

The Scriptures record more than fourteen times that Jesus warned about the coming of false teachers and false prophets. We must remember that any teaching that disregards the power of the resurrection of Jesus Christ, or does not honor Him as being the true Son of the Living God, is of the Antichrist.

God is perfect, and He never changes. God makes no mistakes, and He does not lie.

The teaching of Muhammed does not line up with the Word of God. God didn't change His mind; and the all-powerful Master, Lord God, is more than able to protect His Word from being changed. Is He not able to keep the sun and moon in place? Certainly He can keep His own words from harm or change.

There are many holes in the teaching of Islam. Even though the violent actions of Muslims may contradict what they say, violence is the fruit of what they believe. They may claim to offer peace, but we sure see something much different from peace when we read the newspaper or turn on the television set to watch the news. However, the fault of the violence that is being perpetuated by the Muslims does not just rest with the individual Muslim people. We must remember that they are actually following the ways and former lifestyle of their dead prophet.

Please take a closer, deeper look, and do not fall into their hole!

By contrast, however, if we all followed the life of Jesus, there would be perfect peace, love, joy and all the things we desire that are pure.

He is a just and a loving God, but He also gives us the choice! Sometimes people question why God allows certain things to happen in the world. Mother Teresa answered a question like this in a very simple way when she was once asked the question, "Why doesn't God heal or give us a cure for Aids?" Her reply cut right to the heart of matter when she said, "He did, but it got aborted!"

Every second, people all over the world are making choices. In fact, you, my friend, are making a choice right now about what you will think and do. Will you listen to the voice of the Holy Spirit or your own voice?

I understand the concept of choices. I am faced with them every day, all day long. For example, it seems like the moment I begin to pray, read the Word or listen to a speaker, my mind starts to wander. I begin to think about making dinner, paying bills, what the kids are doing or what I'll do next. Each time this happens, I am presented with a choice. Will I, or will I not, bring my mind back to my Lord in prayer? Will I, or will I not, ponder what He is saying to me through His Word or through the speaker?

We all have many choices to make each day. For example, even deciding what we will wear is a choice, often an important one. When we choose how we will dress, we must ask ourselves, "Is what I am wearing going to affect my brothers and sisters in the Lord in a positive way, or is what I am wearing going to cause someone to stumble?"

Other choices include whether we will answer back with a kind word or with a harsh one. Will we give God what is His or spend the money on ourselves. Will we put healthy, or unhealthy, things in our mouths? What will we choose to hear and see? Will our choices bring us closer to the Lord or will they draw us away from Him?

This all may sound so minor, but there is validity to the statement "if you give the devil an inch, he'll take a mile or two or more." Remember, the enemy comes to steal, kill and destroy.

The Bible teaches us to cast down every vain imagination (See 2 Corinthians 10:5.)

> For although they knew God, they neither glorified him as God nor gave thanks to him, but their thinking became futile and their foolish hearts were darkened.
>
> —ROMANS 1:21

> Do not let anyone who delights in false humility and the worship of angels disqualify you for the prize. Such a person goes into great detail about what he has seen, and his unspiritual mind puffs him up with idle notions.
>
> —COLOSSIANS 2:18

In 2 Corinthians 10:5–6, we are told to not entertain evil. "We demolish arguments and every pretension that sets itself up against the knowledge of God, and we take captive every thought to make it obedient to Christ. And we will be ready to punish every act of disobedience, once your obedience is complete."

Do you realize that every choice we make has a price tag and always involves some kind of pain? This is true for good choices or wrong ones. The pain will entail either the pain of dying to self and the desires of the flesh when we choose to do what is right, or the pain of the consequences of making the wrong choice.

Yes, there is pleasure in sin for a season, but the wages of sin is death.

> Choosing rather to suffer affliction with the people of God, than to enjoy the pleasures of sin for a season;
> —HEBREWS 11:25

> For the wages of sin is death, but the gift of God is eternal life in Christ Jesus our Lord.
> —ROMANS 6:23

> The mind of sinful man is death, but the mind controlled by the Spirit is life and peace.
> —ROMANS 8:6

The more bad choices we make, the more pain we will have: either here, now, later or at the cost of eternity.

I do want to point out, however, that this is really not a testimony on pain. Instead, it is a testimony of God's grace and mercy. Years ago I made very wrong choices, and I was fully aware of them. The Holy Spirit gave me many red flags. But the more we push away His voice, the harder it is to hear Him.

At the time I began turning the wrong way, I knew and loved my Savior, and He was Lord of my life. I was born again in 1972 and was headed into a full-time ministry, singing for Jesus. But I made wrong choices. I let disappointment rule me; I allowed bitterness to take root in my life, and so I began my compromises.

Wouldn't it be wonderful if the enemy would come in through the front door in broad daylight? But this is not the case. The Bible tells us that he comes in like a thief in the night. However, we can recognize our enemy through one very simple way: In Galatians 5, we are told that we will know them by their fruits. Yes, sometimes the enemy appears in sheep's clothing, but remember this: Sheep eat grass; but wolves eat sheep.

> The thief comes only to steal and kill and destroy; I have come that they may have life, and have it to the full.
>
> —JOHN 10:10

> Humble yourselves, therefore, under God's mighty hand, that he may lift you up in due time. Cast all your anxiety on him because he cares for you. Be self-controlled and alert. Your enemy the devil prowls around like a roaring lion looking for someone to devour. Resist him, standing firm in the faith, because you know that your brothers throughout the world are undergoing the same kind of sufferings. And the God of all grace, who called you to his eternal glory in Christ, after you have suffered a little while, will himself restore you and make you strong, firm and steadfast. To him be the power for ever and ever. Amen.
>
> —1 PETER 5:6–11

Jesus is faithful and just, and we can fully trust that in Him all things are possible.

> …being confident of this, that he who began a good work in you will carry it on to completion until the day of Christ Jesus.
>
> —PHILIPPIANS 1:6

> And we know that in all things God works for the good of those who love him, who have been

called according to his purpose. And that He
knows His own and is faithful to keep what is His.
—ROMANS 8:28

All I have is yours, and all you have is mine.
And glory has come to me through them. I will
remain in the world no longer, but they are still in
the world, and I am coming to you. Holy Father,
protect them by the power of your name—the
name you gave me—so that they may be one as
we are one. While I was with them, I protected
them and kept them safe by that name you gave
me. None has been lost except the one doomed to
destruction so that Scripture would be fulfilled.
—JOHN 17:10–12

I walked away from the Lord for many years. I
turned my back on Him completely. I denied Him. I
denied that I even knew Him. I even brought converts
to Islam. I wore the veil of Islam for over two years,
and did everything a good Muslim was supposed to
do. I sold out Jesus for what I thought was "true love."
And I began to worship a man instead of the Lord. My
bad choices bought me much heartache and many
bruises, inside and out.

I tried very hard to work my way into heaven by
serving my husband. His religion taught that I could
only get into heaven by being the best wife possible,
and I bought into that lie. I was told that I could only
enter into heaven if my husband gave his permission.
And what would be my reward? I would be able to
watch him take virgins and young boys and drink wine
until his belly was full. This is the reward that a faithful
wife of a Muslim man looks forward to in the afterlife.
This is also the part that is not initially revealed to a

potential bride for a Muslim man.

Along with this, my earthly rewards were that I lost my family, friends, job and recognition of self-worth. I lost all of these precious blessings from the one-and-only true God because being locked into my husband's house and obeying his every desire was the way I earned the privilege of having my basic, daily needs met by him.

How did I get so deceived? Initially, one would think that any woman with any mind would surely say, "No way!" But the enemy is so subtle; He comes in slowly. This deception took me over little by little, bit by bit. However, it all initially started with my own choice to become embittered and to compromise. So how was I ultimately so deceived even though I had known the Lord Jesus Christ? With every choice I made to compromise, I was choosing to ignore the voice of the Holy Spirit that had once spoken so clearly to my heart and mind. We must remember that every time we make a wrong choice, we lose sensitivity to the Holy Spirit; but each time we listen to and obey His voice, we become more sensitive to the voice of the Holy Spirit.

I made the choice to marry the wrong person, but I will not stand here and tell you that there were never any happy times. If that had been the case, I would never have stayed married for over fifteen years. I am not even blaming my ex-husband for my choices. I knew the truth, and I made the choice to walk away from truth.

There were the joys of the birth of my children and the many things we had, and I saw the world during our travels. But one day I realized I had lost the greatest things—real peace, joy and love—and that I was going to lose out on eternity. When I realized I had lost Jesus, I was presented with another choice; the choice to give up all of the worldly things, even at the possible cost of my life here on this earth. Yes, the price tag was great, but I made my stand for Jesus. And when I took that stand, my husband divorced me and told me that he was going to throw me out into the streets. So instead of bowing to his threats, I made the choice to leave with my children and retreat to our small house. With that choice came delightful peace and the freedom to worship my Lord and Savior. It was well worth the price.

For almost a year, my children and I had to live totally by faith. When I moved out, I had very little money. Of course, the money went quickly because I had to provide for my four children who were all living with me at home. But God's grace was always there.

> And God is able to make all grace abound to you, so that in all things at all times, having all that you need, you will abound in every good work.
> —2 CORINTHIANS. 9:8

> And my God will meet all your needs according to his glorious riches in Christ Jesus.
> —PHILIPPIANS 4:19

These were scriptures we lived by and still do. The miracle of my story is God's grace and His wonderful mercy. I was blessed with a wonderful family that loved the Lord Jesus and never ever gave up praying for me even though I had made the wrong choice. No, I was not a person who was raised in an abusive home. I also had many accomplishments on my own merit, but slowly but surely I was sucked down deeper and deeper into the pit of deception and despair. However, even when I was in that dark place, my parents kept praying for me. So I tell you this, no matter how dark the place where your loves one may seem to be, never give up, never stop praying for them, until you receive that answer to your prayer.

Once, when I was on Arthlene Rippy's show, she said something that really blessed me. She said I was like an example of Israel. . . . They knew God, but walked away . . . and God's mercy was still poured out on them. Her words touch my heart deeply because I had experienced that mercy—and you and your loved ones can too, my friend.

Remember how earlier in my testimony I told about how my mother attended a Bible study for years, and it just so happened that while I moved back to Georgia for a period of four months, I was asked to rent my house to a ladies' group one weekend per month? Little did I know that this was a group of wonderful Christian women. I also didn't know this was the group of women who led the Bible study that my mother had attended for years. My mother had asked them to pray for me many, many times. And now they were there in my house; and as they looked around, they saw a picture of my mother and me. I was the daughter they had prayed for over so many years.

You see, my mother had been praying for me for years, and she had asked others to pray for me. And now these precious women responded to the cry of her heart and the unction of the Holy Spirit and prayed over everything in my house. They took oil and prayed over every picture, over all my clothes, and throughout the whole house.

Did those prayers make a difference? Absolutely! In fact, when I came back to the house, the Holy Spirit began to deal with me so strongly that at one point I really thought I was going to lose my mind. My despair drove me to call a neighbor whom I had heard was a good Christian. That phone call ultimately led me to go to church with her and then come back to Jesus. Does God answer the prayers of a praying mother and family? Yes, indeed!

Also, my parents prayed a special prayer every day for two months, and within those two months my brother and I both came back to Jesus. Before sharing this prayer with you, however, I want to remind you of a few precious scriptures from God's Word.

> Therefore confess your sins to each other and pray for each other so that you may be healed. The prayer of a righteous man is powerful and effective for God's words will never return void.
>
> —JAMES. 5:16

> . . . so is my word that goes out from my mouth: It will not return to me empty, but will accomplish what I desire and achieve the purpose for which I sent it.
>
> —ISAIAH 55:11

> Jesus said to him, "Today salvation has come to this house, because this man, too, is a son of Abraham."
>
> —LUKE 19:9

To me, this passage of Scripture applies to the Muslims.

Many people have asked me how I made it through everything. I know that I shouldn't be alive, but I serve a living God who cares about everything that concerns me. He gave me the faith to keep walking; He gave me the faith to trust Him; and when there was a storm, He gave me the courage to walk through it. I kept walking when I didn't see the end. I kept walking when the tears poured out of my very soul like buckets of water. I kept walking when there was very little to nothing. I kept walking when all my things were taken away. I kept walking when friends turned against me. I kept walking when lies were spread about me. I kept walking when I was spit on, hit, pushed, cursed and hated. I kept walking when it hurt so bad and I felt all alone, knowing that God was still with me and that my feelings had nothing to do with it, knowing that we cannot go by feelings nor can we lean on our own understanding.

I saw that no matter what, whether God's blessings were added or removed from my life, He is still God! I am still learning to count it all JOY, knowing that all things work together for good for those who love the Lord and are called according to His purpose.

The Lord is now not only adding to my life, but also multiplying it. I stand in awe of Him...I find myself running just to keep up with all His blessings, for He is so faithful, and He is truly the God of restoration.

My friend, let your faith rise up: It is time to take back what has been robbed from you. The enemy has been defeated, and Jesus has won! Now it is up to you to make the very important choice of praying for your loved ones. However, first things must be first:

If you have never accepted Jesus as your Lord and Savior, please pray a prayer like this now—

*Lord Jesus, I ask You to forgive me of all my sins. Come into my heart. Cleanse me and make Yours. Lord Jesus, I know I can never be good enough to get into heaven. I know that it is by grace that I am being saved. I thank You, Lord Jesus, for dying for me on calvary. I believe You are the Son of God. I believe the whole Bible to be Your words. Thank You, Lord Jesus. Please be not only my Savior, but my Lord as well. Please take my life and use it for Your glory. Thank You, Jesus, for loving me while I was still a sinner. In Your name, I ask these things. Amen!*

For those who are coming back home to the Lord:

*Lord Jesus, I am sorry for turning my back on You. I ask that You please forgive me. Please fill me like never before with Your Holy Spirit. Take me back into Your loving arms, Lord Jesus. I ask You to empower me and renew my first love for You, Jesus. Make me hungry for You, Jesus, and for Your Word. Use me ,Lord Jesus. Take my mess and make it useable for Your glory. I know that all things will work out for the good for those who love You, Jesus. Thank You, Lord, that You were always near me. I love You, Jesus. Thank You, Jesus, for bringing me back to You. In Your name, I pray. Amen.*

Now I want to share the prayer that my parents prayed faithfully for me and my brother. It is time for you to take back your loved ones. If you have a lost loved one, I want you to pray this prayer with me. This is a copy of the prayer that my parents prayed for me and within two months I found my way back to Jesus!

For those who are ready to defeat the strongholds that have been binding your loved ones...

*"In the name of Jesus Christ, I bind_____'s body, soul and spirit to the will and purposes of God for his/her life. I bind _____'s mind, will and emotions to the will of God. I bind him/her to the truth and to the blood of Jesus. I bind his/her*

*mind to the mind of Christ, that the very thoughts, feelings and purposes of His heart would be within his/her thoughts. I bind _____'s feet to the path of righteousness that his/her steps would be steady and sure. I bind him/her to the work of the cross with all of its mercy, grace, love, forgiveness and dying to self.*

*"I loose every old, wrong, ungodly pattern of thinking, attitude, idea, desire, belief, motivation, habit and behavior from him/her. I tear down, crush, smash and destroy every stronghold associated with these things. I loose any stronghold in his/her life that has been justifying and protecting hard feelings against anyone. I loose the strongholds of unforgiveness, fear and distrust from him/her.*

*"I loose the power and effects of deceptions and lies from him/her. I loose the confusion and blindness of the god of this world from_____'s mind that has kept him/her from seeing the light of the gospel of Jesus Christ. I call forth every precious word of Scripture that has ever entered into his/her mind and heart that it would rise up in power within him/her.*

*"In the name of Jesus, I loose the power and effects of any harsh or hard words [words curses] spoken to, about or by _____. I loose all generational bondage's and associated strongholds from_____. I loose all effects and bondage's from him/her that may have been caused by mistakes I have made. Father, in the name of Jesus, I crush, smash and destroy generational bondage's of any kind from mistakes made at any point between generations. I destroy them right here, right now. They will not bind and curse any more*

47

*members of this family.*

*"I bind the strong man, Satan, that may spoil his house taking back every material and spiritual possession he has wrongfully taken from_____.*

*I loose the enemies influence over every part of his/her body, soul, and spirit. I loose, crush, smash and destroy every evil device he may try to bring into his/her sphere of influence during this day and the days to follow.*

*"I bind and loose these things in Jesus' name. He has given me the keys and the authority to do so, in His name, Jesus. Now Lord Jesus we thank You for the truth that will set them free and, Jesus, You said that wherever two or more are gathered and what we agreed on it shall be done. We are all standing in agreement here right now together for the salvation of every name that has been called out. And, Father God, You have said that Your desire is that none should perish. Thank You again. In Jesus name. And we will never touch Your glory, Lord. It all belongs to You. Amen and amen. As Jesus said on the cross, 'It is finished!' Praise You, Jesus."*

# PART 2

# WHERE HAVE ALL
# THE WEDDING BELLS GONE?

Instead of being led down church aisles, many American women are being led to the mosque by Middle Eastern men who have captivated them. A mosque is a building used by Muslims as a place of Islamic worship. Twenty-five years ago this would have been a rare event in the United States. However, Islam has become one of the fastest growing religions in the world and it is no longer just "overseas." It has reached our borders and shorelines, and Muslim men are capturing the hearts of our mothers, sisters and daughters.

# KNOWING YOUR PURSUER

Middle Eastern men come to the United States in search of not only of their fortunes, but also of brides. They are usually very intelligent, come from wealthy backgrounds and know how to get what they want. They are charming, romantic, passionate, virile and seemingly sincere. They wine, dine and woo women into their webs. The sad part of their deceit is that they have the appearance of a man who loves God, holds high moral values and wants a decent home and family. When asked, they will tell you that they believe in God, the Bible, Jesus, heaven, hell, angels, prophets and the day of judgment.

Why do these men come here and go after the good Christian women rather than their own Arabic women? Because they are taught that if they marry a Christian or Jewish woman, Allah, their god, will love them more because of the possibility of conversion! It has also been said to me and to other women that "If the Muslim man cannot take us by force then they will take us through marriage."

The Hadith below gives proof of this belief.

*Volume 7, Book 62, Number 8:*

*Narrated 'Umar bin Al-Khattab:*

**The Prophet said, "The rewards (of deeds) are according to the intention, and everybody will get the**

*reward for what he has intended. So whoever emigrated for Allah's and His Apostle's sake, his emigration was for Allah and His Apostle; and whoever emigrated for worldly benefits, or to marry a woman, then his emigration was for the thing for what he emigrated for."*

# CAUGHT IN THEIR WEB

How do they try to trap women? It seems a bit medieval for a person to be trapped. But the reality is that it happens every day. Women are courted by Muslim men, form deep loving relationships with them and are then asked to marry them.

Why wouldn't a woman believe and trust her fiancé? The fact is, however, that Muslim men are taught that Allah loves those who outwit (lie) the best. Most of the courtships are very fast. In some cases, a couple may get married within a day or two, but most within a few months. It is rare for a Muslim man to wait a year before he marries. Let's not forget that another motivation for these quick marriages may be a Green Card for U. S. citizenship.

Below is proof for outwitting or, rather, lying:

*(6303) Humaid b. `Abd al-Rahman b. `Auf reported that his mother Umm Kiltbum... as saying that she heard Allah's Messenger (may peace be upon him) as saying: A liar is not one who tries to bring reconciliation amongst people and speaks good (in order to avert dispute), or he conveys good. Ibn Shihab said he did not hear that exemption was granted in anything what the people speak as lie but in three cases: in battle, for bringing reconciliation amongst persons and the narration of the words of the husband to his*

*wife, and the narration of the words of a wife to her husband (in a twisted form in order to bring reconciliation between them)." (Note: all words are as they appear in the text; Sahih Muslim, p.1374, #6303).*

*"`Ali said: Whenever I narrate to you anything from the Messenger of Allah (may peace be upon him) believe it to be absolutely true as falling from the sky is dearer to me than that of attributing anything to him (the Holy Prophet) which he never said. When I talk to you of anything which is between me and you (there might creep some error in it) for battle is an outwitting." (Vol. 2, p. 523f).*

*"Battle is an outwitting." Hadrat 'Ali took an oath in order to make it clear that this narration from the Holy Prophet (may peace be upon him) about the Khwarij is not a piece of outwitting but a genuine statement of fact as told by the Messenger of Allah (may peace be upon him)." (Vol. 2, ft. #1452)*

*These were not the type of lies which are counted as serious sin in religion. These may be called tauriya or double-entendre which means using a word, an expression or a phrase, which has an obvious meaning and intending thereby another meaning to which it applies, but which is contrary to the obvious one." (Vol. 1, ft. 402, English version)*

# THE WEDDING CONVERSION

In some cases, a woman does not even know she is being given in matrimony. For those who don't know they are being married (and converted), a woman is told that the only way his family will like her is if she goes to a religious ceremony with them. For those who do know they are being married, a common line used by Muslim men is "that in order for the marriage to mean something special to them and the only way that the marriage will work," is if they are married in the mosque. The other way they trick the woman is to tell them that the ceremony is only for engagement.

At the ceremony, the "groom" is not usually near his "bride." In fact, he is on the other side of the room that has in some way been divided by a curtain, or he is in a different room altogether. Women are together and men are together during the ceremony. The woman is asked to repeat many things in Arabic. She usually does not have anyone with her, such as her friends or family, nor is there anyone available to translate the Arabic for her. The Muslim women just nudge the bride and tell her to just say "yes." After all is said and done, the new bride walks out with a new husband (sometimes not knowing she is married), a new Muslim family, a new Muslim name, a new religion, and unfortunately, no marital rights. She has now become her new husband's possession.

# THE HONEYMOON

What should a woman expect after she has married a Muslim man? Basically, she has the right to remain silent: EVERYTHING SHE SAYS WILL BE USED AGAINST HER. The Hadith below is an excellent representation of what a woman may expect once she is married to a Muslim man.

The Hadiths are collections of the teachings and traditions of the (false) Prophet Muhammed. The Qur'an sets the guidelines for the Muslims, the Hadiths demonstrate those guidelines in actual practice.

*Volume 7, Book 62, Number 32:*

*Narrated Sahl bin Sad: Allah's Apostle said, "If at all there is bad omen, it is the horse, the woman, and the house."*

Man's status is so much higher than woman's that no sacrifice on the woman's part will ever gain her her full right in relation to a man. Even in our own time (1985) a Muslim writer, Ahmad Zaky Tuffaha, seriously and reverently quotes the following Hadith:

*"If a woman offered one of her breasts to be cooked and the other to be roasted, she still will fall short of fulfilling her obligations to her husband. And besides that if she disobeys her husband even for a twinkling of an eye, she would be thrown in the lowest part of Hell, except she*

*repents and turns back." [48]*

Although this Hadith is not mentioned in Bukhari, it is consistent with the other Hadith quoted by Bukhari.

It is a noble sacrifice for a man to share his life with the woman as described in Bukhari's sound Hadith; she being deficient in mind, religion, and gratitude. It is condescension on the part of the man to spend his life with her. She can not repay this favour, no matter what sacrifice she makes.

Indeed, the rights of the husband are so vast that:

*"If blood, suppuration, and pus, were to pour from the husband's nose and the wife licked it with her tongue, she would still never be able to fulfil his rights over her." [49]*

This Hadith is repeated, also with great reverence, five times by commentator Imam Suyuti who is regarded as one of the greatest of all Muslim scholars.

(Source:

http://debate.domini.org/newton/womeng.html)

# THE HUSBAND

Muslim men are, to some, considered the frightening pinnacle of male chauvinism, where women are viewed on the same level as slaves to the man. Let's take this opportunity to go over what is expected from a wife as stated in the Islamic Hadith's below. Take note that in Islam men are superior to women in every way.

*"...And women shall have rights similar to the rights against them, according to what is equitable; but men have a degree (superiority) over them." (Surah 2:228)*

*"Fair in the eyes of men is the love of things they covet: women and sons, heaped-up hordes of gold and silver; horses..." (Surah 3:14)*

*If a Muslim man touches a woman (even his wife) before praying, he is considered unclean for prayer. (Surah 4:43)*

*"...And say to the believing women...that they should draw veils over their bosoms and not display their beauty." (Surah 24:31)*

*"I have not seen anyone more deficient in intelligence and religion than women." (Al Bukhary Vol. 2:541)*

*"After me I have not left any affliction more harmful to men than women." (Al Bukhary Vol. 7:33)*

# HIS BEFORE YOURS

*'Abd al-Malik (RA) said: "When 'Awf ibn Muhallim al-Shaybani, one of the most highly respected leaders of the Arab nobility during the jahiliyyah, married his daughter Umm Iyas to al-Harith ibn 'Amr al-Kindi, she was made ready to be taken to the groom, then her mother, Umamah came into her, to advise her and said:*

*Take from me ten qualities, which will be a provision and a reminder for you.*

*The first and second of them are: be content in his company, and listen to and obey him, for contentment brings peace of mind, and listening to and obeying one's husband pleases Allah.*

*The third and fourth of them are: make sure that you smell good and look good; he should not see anything ugly in you, and he should not smell anything but a pleasant smell from you. Kohl is the best kind of beautification to be found, and water is better than the rarest perfume.*

*The fifth and sixth of them are: prepare his food on time, and keep quiet when he is asleep, for raging hunger is like a burning flame, and disturbing his sleep will make him angry.*

*The seventh and eighth of them are: take care of his servants (or employees) and children, and take care of his wealth, for taking care of his wealth shows that you appreciate him, and taking care of his children and servants shows good management.*

*The ninth and tenth of them are: never disclose any of his secrets, and never disobey any of his orders, for if you disclose any of his secrets you will never feel safe from his possible betrayal, and if you disobey him, his heart will be filled with hatred towards you. 'Be careful, O my daughter, of showing joy in front of him when he is upset, and do not show sorrow in front of him when he is happy, because the former shows a lack of judgment whilst the latter will make him unhappy.*

*'Show him as much honor and respect as you can, and agree with him as much as you can, so that he will enjoy your companionship and conversation.*

*'Know, O my daughter, that you will not achieve what you would like to until you put his pleasure before your own, and his wishes before yours, in whatever you like and dislike. And may Allah choose what is best for you and protect you." (Jamharah Khutab al-'Arab, 1/145)*

# THE WIFE SHOULD SEEK THE PLEASURE OF HER HUSBAND

*"What is obligatory upon the woman is that she seeks the pleasure of her husband, and avoids angering him, and does not refuse him whenever he wants her.*

*The woman must also know that she is like a slave to her husband, so she should not do anything affecting herself or her husband's wealth except with his permission.*

*She should give precedence to his rights over her rights, and the rights of his relatives over the rights of her relatives, and she should keep herself clean and be ready for him to enjoy her.*

*She should not boast at his expense of her beauty, nor rebuke him for any ugliness found in him. The woman must also be always modest and reserved in the presence of her husband, lower her eyes in front of him, obey his commands, remain silent when he speaks, keep far away from everything which angers him, avoid treachery when he is absent, with regard to his bed, his wealth and his house.*

*She should ensure that her aroma is pleasant, be accustomed to using musk and perfume and cleaning her mouth with miswaak.*

*She should be constant in adorning herself in his*

*presence and not when he is absent.*

*She should treat his family and relatives honorably, and consider something small from him as something great."*

*I command you to treat women kindly. Woman has been created from a rib (the rib is crooked), and the most crooked part of the rib is the upper region. If you try to make it straight you will break it, and if you leave it as it is, it will remain curved. So treat women kindly." by Al-Bukhari (18)*

# DAILY MAINTENANCE

Below are the requirements for a wife's daily needs to be met:

*The follower of Imam Ibn Hanbal said, The wife's daily maintenance is due upon the husband if the wife surrenders herself to her husband completely . . . for the daily maintenance is given to the woman in return for the husband's sexual enjoyment, so when the wife surrenders herself her daily maintenance is obligatory as long as she had reached nine years old. . . . so if she was physically and surrendered herself for the enjoyment of the husband but without sexual intercourse, she has no right for the daily maintenance.*

*So if the wife refuses to surrender herself so that the husband might have sex with her, her daily maintenance is denied. So if she then has a problem that prevents her from having sex with her husband, but surrenders herself to her husband after that, her daily maintenance is not given to her as long as she is sick, as a punishment for her because she refused to surrender to her husband when she was well."*

Ibid, pages 497–499

*The follower of imam Shafi'i said: "The conditions of the man's maintenance for the women are as follows:*

*1) She must avail herself by offering herself to him, such as saying to him 'I surrender myself to you'. The important thing is that she must notify him in advance that she is ready for his meeting with her, and of his entrance upon her no right of maintenance, even if she does not notify him that she is ready, she has no right of maintenance, even if she does not refuse his request to meet with her. So maintenance is conditional upon the woman's notification to her husband that she is ready for his meeting anytime he wishes. So, if she be denied.*

*2) She must be capable of having sexual intercourse. If she was a small girl, that cannot cope with intercourse, she is not entitled to the maintenance.*

*3) She must not be rebellious, that is, disobeying her husband, which can take the form of preventing him from enjoying her by refusing his touch and his kisses and refusing to have sex.*

*If she denies him any of the above, her maintenance will be canceled for that day, because maintenance is due day by day. . . . and the rebelliousness of one day cancels his provision for clothing her for a whole season.*

*The followers from Imam Malik said: The condition for the man's maintenance to the woman is that she should avail herself to the man for the sexual intercourse, so that if he requested it from her she would not refuse. Otherwise, she would have no right to the maintenance.*

# SUPPORT

If a man becomes angry with his wife, he has the right to not provide for her. In Islam, there is no such law as community property between the husband and wife. Hence, the wife must rely on the support of her husband on a daily basis. However, as the following indicates, there numerous grounds on which the husband can refuse to provide support for his wife:

*Volume 4, page 495*

***The support of the women (nafaqa) is obligatory on the man in return for the women being locked up in the man's house, and for being exclusively his, The Hanafites said:***

***There is no support for the women if she is—***

***1) Rebellious (Nashiz) that is the woman who goes outside the house of the husband without his permission and without a justifiable reason, or refuses surrendering herself to him so she does not enter his house. But if she refuses to have sex with him (even though that is unlawful) that refusal is not a reason for stopping her support because the qualifying reason for the support does exist and that is her being locked up in his house.***

***2) The renegade woman.***

***3) The woman who obeys the husband's son or father or kisses either with lust or anything that***

*might put her relation with her husband on a prohibited degree.*

*4) The woman whose marriage contract is imperfect, and the woman who had sex with someone by mistake, the man thinking she was his wife.*

*5) The wife who is too young too have sex. [the Islamic law knows no minimum age for a legal marriage. (Encyclopedia of Islam)].*

*6) The wife who is imprisoned, even if she is innocent, if can not have access to her (as a wife).*

*7) The sick wife who, due to severe illness, did not move after the ceremony to the husband's house, because she did not surrender herself to her husband.*

*8) The wife who was raped by another man.*

*9) The wife who goes to perform pilgrimage....There is no support for her because she is not locked up. [Volume 4, pages 495–497]*

# SEX

The wife: A sex object. *"...your wives are as a tilth (a field to be ploughed) unto you, so approach your tilth when or how ye will." (Surah 2:223)*

*Volume 7, Book 62, Number 18: Narrated 'Ursa:* **The Prophet asked Abu Bakr for 'Aisha's hand in marriage. Abu Bakr said "But I am your brother." The Prophet said, "You are my brother in Allah's religion and His Book, but she (Aisha) is lawful for me to marry."**

*Volume 7, Book 62, Number 17: Narrated Jabir bin 'Abdullah:* **When I got married, Allah's Apostle said to me, "What type of lady have you married?" I replied, "I have married a matron' He said, "Why, don't you have a liking for the virgins and for fondling them?" Jabir also said: Allah's Apostle said, "Why didn't you marry a young girl so that you might play with her and she with you?'**

*"Narrated Jabir: Jews used to say; if one has sexual intercourse with his wife from the back, then she will deliver a squint-eyed child. So this verse was revealed: 'your wives are a tilth unto you, so approach your tilth when and how ye will" (whether in a natural or unnatural way). (Al Bukhary Vol. 6:51)*

*Volume 7, Book 62, Number 6: Narrated Anas:* **The Prophet I used to go round (have sexual relations with) all his wives in one night, and he had nine wives.**

# THE HUSBAND'S RIGHT
# TO BEAT THE WIFE

According to the Qur'an, a man has the right and responsibility to admonish his wife, to desert her sexually and to beat her in order to correct any rebelliousness in her behavior. The wife-beating issue is just another attempt by Muslim apologists to sugarcoat Islam in the West. However, the following comes from their Hadith. I am amazed at how modern scholars are trying to alter the meaning of these and are actually getting away with it. Maybe the staunch Muslim scholars don't mind as long as it brings in converts—sorta like the old "bait-and-switch" sales pitch.

### BEATING YOUR WIFE...

*The Prophet said: "When one of you inflicts a beating, he should avoid striking the face."*
*(Narrated Abu Huraira)*
*The man according to the Qur'an has the responsibility to admonish his wife, and the right to desert her sexually, and to beat her to correct any rebelliousness in her behavior.*
*The translator of Mishkrat Al_Massabih wrote in a footnote of Fatwa by Qazi Khan that said beating the wife mildly is allowed in four cases:*

*When she wears fineries though wanted by the husband,*

*When she is called for sexual intercourse and she refuses without any lawful excuse,*

*When she is ordered to take a bath (to clean herself) from impurities for prayer and she refuses and*

*When she goes abroad without permission of her husband." (60)*

*In another footnote the translator of Mishkat Al-Masabih said,*

*"No wife shall refuse her husband what he wants from her except on religious grounds (i.e. —at the time of menstrual flow or fasting).* Some theologians regard the refusal as unlawful as the husband may get enjoyment from his wife in other ways, by embracing, kissing, etc. *"The duty of the wife is to give him comforts in his bed whenever he wants her," (61)* This beating is the husband's unquestionable right.

Ibn Kathir in his commentary mentioned a Hadith on the authority of zal Ash'ath Ibn as-Qays who was visiting Omar and at the time.

*"Omar took his wife and beat her, then said to Ash'arth: Memorize three things from me.*

*Which I memorized from the prophet who said: "The man is not to be asked why he beat his wife.."(62)*

## THE MARRIAGE CONTRACT

The marriage contract, like most of the thoughts on women, centers on the sexual part of the relationship. A man is expected to take care of his wife as far as providing her with food, clothing, shelter and the like. A woman, on the other hand, is expected to obey and sexually submit herself to her husband whenever he wishes it, no matter what her age or circumstance. The husband only has to provide for the wife as long as she is able to give him what he wants, whenever and wherever he wants it. We will discuss this in the next chapters.

*"As to those women on whose part ye fear disloyalty and ill-conduct, admonish them, refuse to share their beds, beat them..." (Surah 4:34)*

*Volume 7, Book 63, Number 209:*
*Narrated Nafi':..(22)*

*Whenever Ibn "Umar was asked about marrying a Christian lady or a Jewess, he would say: "Allah has made it unlawful for the believers to marry ladies who ascribe partners in worship to Allah, and I do not know of a greater thing, as regards to ascribing partners in worship, etc.,, to Allah, than that a lady should say that Jesus is her Lord although he is just one of Allah's slaves."*

*"The marriage contract is designed by the legislator so that the husband may benefit from the sexual organ of the woman and the rest of her body for the purpose of pleasure. As such the husband owns by the marriage contract, this exclusive benefit." (112)*

*"The accepted understanding in the different schools of jurisprudence, is that what has been contracted in marriage is for the benefit of the man from the woman, no the opposite. The followers of Imam Malik declares the marriage contract is a contract of ownership of benefit of the sexual organ of the woman and the rest of her body."*

*The followers of Imam Shafi'i said: "The most accepted view is that what is been contracted upon is the woman, that is the benefit derived from her sexual organ. Others said, "What has been contracted is both the man and the woman. So according to the first opinion the wife can not demand sex from her hus-*

*band because it is his right (not hers), and according to the second opinion she can demand to have sex with him."*

*The followers of Imam Abu Hanifa said: "The right of the sexual pleasures belongs to the man, not the woman, by that it is meant that the man has the right to force the woman to gratify himself sexually. She on the other hand does not have the right to force him to have sex with her except once (in a lifetime). But he must, from a religious point of view, have sex with her to protect her from being morally corrupt." (113) (23)*

# POLYGAMY

It is not unusual for a Muslim man to have more than one wife. In fact, he can have up to four wives at one time. Muhammed had many wives at one time, which even included a small girl.

*A man may marry up to four wives at one time. "Marry women of your choice, two, or three, or four." (Surah 4:3)*

*Volume 4, page 89*

*"For if a man purchases a slave girl, the purchase contract includes his right to have sex with her." This contract is primarily to own her and secondarily to enjoy her sexually."*

*Volume 2, page 33*

*"Since among Arabs passion is an overpowering aspect of their nature, the need of their pious men to have sex has been found to be the more intense. And for the purpose of emptying the hearts to the worship of God they have been allowed to have sex with women slaves if at some time they should fear that this passion will [cause] them to commit adultery. Though it is true that such action could lead to the birth of a child that will be a slave, which is a form of destruction . . . yet enslaving a child is a lighter offense than the destruction of religious belief. For enslaving the new born is a temporary thing but by committing adultery eternity is lost."*

# CHILDREN

So much could be shared about the children. This one subject alone could be a book. For instance, Muslims believe the treatment a child receives is dependent on the age of a child: From birth to ages 6... Play with them; Ages 7-13...break them; Ages 14-21... build them; and after Age 21... try to be their friend. Also, Islam says to teach your children three things before the age of five...1) how to swim, 2) how to ride a horse, and 3) how to use a gun.

An interesting fact about children is that a child's resemblance to the father is a sign of the mother's love for the father. In other words, if junior is born looking like dad, then Mom truly loves Dad. But what if Junior doesn't look like Dad?

*Volume 6, Book 60, Number 7:*

*Narrated Anas:*

*'Abdullah bin Salam heard the news of the arrival of Allah's Apostle (at Medina) while he was on a farm collecting its fruits. So he came to the Prophet and said, "I will ask you about three things which nobody knows unless he be a prophet. Firstly, what is the first portent of the Hour? What is the first meal of the people of Paradise? And what makes a baby look like its father or mother?'. The Prophet said, "Just now Gabriel has informed me about that." 'Abdullah said,*

*"Gabriel?" The Prophet said, "Yes." 'Abdullah said, "He, among the angels is the enemy of the Jews." On that the Prophet recited this Holy Verse:—*

*"Whoever is an enemy to Gabriel (let him die in his fury!) for he has brought it (i.e. Qur'an) down to your heart by Allah's permission." (2.97) Then he added, "As for the first portent of the Hour, it will be a fire that will collect the people from the East to West. And as for the first meal of the people of Paradise, it will be the caudite (i.e. extra) lobe of the fish liver. And if a man's discharge proceeded that of the woman, then the child resembles the father, and if the woman's discharge proceeded that of the man, then the child resembles the mother." On hearing that, 'Abdullah said, "I testify that None has the right to be worshipped but Allah, and that you are the Apostle of Allah, O, Allah's Apostle; the Jews are liars, and if they should come to know that I have embraced Islam, they would accuse me of being a liar." In the meantime some Jews came (to the Prophet) and he asked them, "What is 'Abdullah's status amongst you?" They replied, "He is the best amongst us, and he is our chief and the son of our chief." The Prophet said, "What would you think if 'Abdullah bin Salam embraced Islam?" They replied, "May Allah protect him from this!" Then 'Abdullah came out and said, "I testify that None has the right to be worshipped but Allah and that Muhammed is the Apostle of Allah." The Jews then said, "Abdullah is the worst of us and the son of the worst of us," and disparaged him. On that 'Abdullah said, "O Allah's Apostle! This is what I was afraid of!"*

In Islam, children must be raised according to their Muslim father's religion. If the couple divorces, the husband gets custody of the children and the woman will not be able to see the children again. If the couple resides in the United States, there is a fear that the children will be abducted and taken to an Islamic country. There is no such thing as visitation rights in Islam, where the woman has no rights to her children at all.

Another obstacle is the fact that if a woman has agreed to raise the children in the Islamic religion, she may have a court battle on her hands, even in the U.S.

*The Sharia (Islamic Law) states that in mixed marriages "the children will follow the better of the two religions of their parents," which in your case is Islam. The Qur'an states that Islam is the only true religion. "The religion before God is Islam." (Surah 3:19) Non-Muslims cannot act as protectors to Muslims. "O, ye who believe; take not for friends (protectors) unbelievers rather than believers." (Surah 4:144)*

## CHILDREN MAY ALSO BE BEATEN

*Fiqh-us-Sunnah, Fiqh 1.80:*
*Although it is not obligatory for a child to pray, it is a must that his guardian order him to do so when he is seven, and he should beat him if he does not pray after he reaches the age of ten. And have them sleep separately. A minor should practice praying until he reaches puberty.*

## OTHER HADITHS ABOUT CHILDREN

*Volume 7, Book 69, Number 527:*
*Narrated Jabir bin 'Abdullah:*
*Allah's Apostle said, "When night falls (or when it is evening), stop your children from going out, for the devils spread out at that time. But when an hour of the night has passed, release them and close the doors and*

*mention Allah's Name, for Satan does not open a closed door. Tie the mouth of your water-skin and mention Allah's Name; cover your containers and utensils and mention Allah's Name. Cover them even by placing something across it, and extinguish your lamps."*

*Volume 7, Book 71, Number 599:*

*Narrated Anas: that he was asked about the wages of the one who cups others. He said, 'Allah's Apostle was cupped by Abd Taiba, to whom he gave two Sa of food and interceded for him with his masters who consequently reduced what they used to charge him daily. Then the Prophet s said, "The best medicines you may treat yourselves with are cupping and sea incense.' He added, "You should not torture your children by treating tonsillitis by pressing the tonsils or the palate with the finger, but use incense."*

*Volume 8, Book 80, Number 731:*

*Narrated Ibn 'Abbas:*

*(During the early days of Islam), the inheritance used to be given to one's offspring and legacy used to be bequeathed to the parents, then Allah cancelled what He wished from that order and decreed that the male should be given the equivalent of the portion of two females, and for the parents one-sixth for each of them, and for one's wife one-eighth (if the deceased has children) and one-fourth (if he has no children), for one's husband one-half (if the deceased has no children) and one-fourth (if she has children)."*

*Book 010, Number 3831: Rumaid reported that Anas b. Malik (Allah be pleased with him) has asked about the earnings of a cupper. Then (the above-mentioned Hadith was reported but with this addition) that he said: The best treatment which you get is cupping. or aloeswood and do not torture your children by pressing their uvula.*

## CHILDREN FROM A PREVIOUS MARRIAGE

A man does not have to accept children from a previous marriage, especially if that child takes up too much of the mother's time and body. Remember, the husband has all rights to the woman. If an infant is nursing, the husband can demand that his wife stop feeding that baby and instead tend to his needs.

*Hanafites Volume 4, page 488*

**The husband has the right to prevent his wife from looking after and breast feeding her baby from her previous husband, (if she was living in the husband's house), because that will make her too busy to attend to the husband, and it will affect her beauty and cleanliness, all these are the rights of the husband alone.**

## ADOPTION

In Islam, there is no adoption! This is not lawful in the Muslim religion.

*Book 025, Number 5323:*

**Jabir b. 'Abdullah reported: A child was born in the house of a person amongst us, and he gave him the name of Qasim. We said: We will not allow you (to give the name) to your child as Qasim (and thus adopt the kunya of Abu'l-Qasim) and coal your eyes. He (that person) came to Allah's Apostle (may peace be upon him) and made a mention of that to him, whereupon he said: Call your son 'Abd al-Rahman.**

# THE FUTURE

Before we move on, the best advice I can give you regarding marrying someone outside of your faith is found in the Bible: "Be ye not unequally yoked together with unbelievers: for what fellowship hath righteousness with unrighteousness? And what communion hath light with darkness?" (2 Cor. 6:14).

For a Muslim marriage the picture is even bleaker still. Should you survive your Muslim husband, and his wealth is in an Islamic country, the Islamic law applies. The wife who has not converted to Islam gets nothing. The wife who has converted to Islam gets very little. According to the Qur'an, a wife does not inherit all of her husband's wealth. Instead, if the husband dies and he leaves no children, she gets a fourth of his wealth; and his parents, brothers, uncles and other extended family members will get the rest. If the deceased husband leaves children, then the wife gets an eighth and the children get the rest; the male child gets double the portion of the female.

*"In what ye leave, their (wives) share is a fourth if you leave no children; but if you leave a child, they (wives) get an eighth; after payment of legacies and debts." (Surah 4:12)*

A future with a god that loves conditionally also means a future with a man with whom everything is conditional.

*Volume 5, Book 58, Number 127:*

*Narrated Al-Bara:*

**I heard the Prophet saying (or the Prophet said), "None loves the Ansar but a believer, and none hates them but a hypocrite. So Allah will love him who loves them, and He will hate him who hates them."**

# HEAVEN IS FOR THE MAN

The Islamic "Paradise," or *Jannat,* was invented by Muhammed to bribe the Arabs into committing hideous crimes by promising them the materialistic things they couldn't obtain in the harsh desert. The "Paradise" contains six important items: Beautiful virgins, young boys, water, wine, fruits and wealth.

*Displaying Hadith 1 through 3 of 3 Hadith(s) found. (3 Hadith(s) displayed).*

*004.054.476 - Beginning of Creation - Narrated Abu Huraira*

**The Prophet said, "The first batch (of people) who will enter Paradise will be (glittering) like the full moon, and the batch next to them will be (glittering) like the most brilliant star in the sky. Their hearts will be as if the heart of a single man, for they will have neither enmity nor jealousy amongst themselves; everyone will have two wives from the houris, (who will be so beautiful, pure and transparent that) the marrow of the bones of their legs will be seen through the bones and the flesh."**

*Surah 37. as-Saaffaat*

**40. But the sincere (and devoted) servants of Allah 41. For them is a Sustenance Determined 42. Fruits (Delights) and they (shall enjoy) honor and dignity. 43. In Gardens of Felicity. 44. Facing each other on**

*Thrones (of dignity): 45. Round will be passed to them a Cup from a clear-flowing fountain 46. Crystal-white of a taste delicious to those who drink (thereof) 47. Free from headiness; nor will they suffer intoxication there from. 48. And beside them will be chaste women; restraining their glances with big eyes (of wonder and beauty) 49. As if they were (delicate) eggs closely guarded. 50. Then they will turn to one another and question one another. 51. One of them will start the talk and say: "I had an intimate companion (on the earth) 52. "Who used to say `What! Art thou amongst those who bear witness to the truth (of the Message)? 53. "`When we die and become dust and bones shall we indeed receive rewards and punishments?'" 54. (A voice) said: "Would ye like to look down?"*

# YOUNG BOYS AND VIRGINS

Homosexuality is widely practiced in Islamic countries. Muhammed pleased his homosexual followers by promising the pre-pubescent boys in "Paradise." So, after committing plunder, loot, rape and murder in this life, the followers of Islam were told they would be "rewarded" with untouched virginal youths who are fresh like pearls.

Here below are the Qur'an verses that refer to the young boys:

*52:24 Round about them will serve, to them, boys (handsome) as pearls well-guarded.*

*56:12 "round about them will serve boys of perpetual freshness."*

*76:19 And round about them will serve boys of perpetual freshness: if thou seest them, thou wouldst think them scattered pearls.*

Also, Below is an example of an Arabic poem called "Perfumed Garden" by Abu Nuwas, which praises homosexuality:

*O the joy of sodomy!*

*So now be sodomites, you Arabs.*

*Turn not away from it—therein is wondrous pleasure.*

*Take some coy lad with kiss-curls twisting on his temple and ride as he stands like some gazelle standing to her mate.*

*A lad whom all can see girt with sword and belt not like your whore who has to go veiled.*

*Make for smooth-faced boys and do your very best to mount them, for women are the mounts of the devils.*

# THE WIFE CAN ONLY
# GO TO HEAVEN
# BY WAY OF HER HUSBAND

It is said in the Muslim religion that a woman can only get to "Paradise" through her husband. So, if he is not happy with her when she dies, she is believed to suffer in the pits of hell.

Islam also says that the majority of people in hell are women:

**Muhammed said, "I was shown the Hell-fire and that the majority of its dwellers are women."**

*This Hadith can be found in:*

*SaHeeH Bukhari: 29, 304, 1052, 1462, 3241, 5197, 5198, 6449, 6546 (FatH Al-Bari's numbering system)*

**"I stood at the gate of Paradise and saw that the majority of the people who entered it were the poor, while the wealthy were stopped at the gate (for the accounts). But the companions of the Fire were ordered to be taken to the Fire. Then I stood at the gate of the Fire and saw that the majority of those who entered it were women." This is what Muhammed said.**

*This Hadith is found in SaHeeH Bukhari: 5196, 6547 (FatH Al-Bari's numbering system) SaHeeH Muslim: 2736 (Abd Al-BaQi's numbering system)*

*Musnad AHmad: 21275, 21318 (IHya' Al-Turath's*

*numbering system)*

"*I came to Allah's Messenger (SAW) for some need, so he asked, 'You there! Are you married?' I replied, 'Yes.' He then asked, 'How are you towards your husband?' She responded, 'I do not fall short in his service except with regard to what I am unable to do.' He said, 'Then look to your standing with him, for indeed he is your Paradise and your Fire.'*" (Sahih, *reported by al-Haadim and others)*

**Allah's Messenger (SAW) said, "Allah will not look at a woman who is not thankful to her husband and she cannot do without him."**

# DIVORCE

*I divorce you 3x!*

Women are considered to be simple-minded and worthless. Islam allows a man to divorce his wife by oral announcement; the wife has no such right. If a man states "I divorce you" three times to his wife's face, he considers himself legally divorced. Also, a woman is not entitled to any of the husband's possessions, including his children.

*Islam allows a man to divorce his wife by oral announcement, the wife has no such right. ". . . divorce is permissible twice." (Surah 2:229)*

*When a husband has pronounced divorce three times on his wife, she then may not lawfully remarry her husband until she has married and been divorced by another man (including having sexual intercourse with him). "So if a husband divorces his wife he cannot after that, remarry her until after she has married another husband, and he has divorced her." (Surah 2:230)*

*"As to those women on whose part ye fear disloyalty and ill-conduct, admonish them, refuse to share their beds, beat them." (Surah 4:34)*

# THE HADITHS

The Hadiths are collections of the traditions of the Muhammed. While the Qur'an sets the guidelines for Muslims, the Hadiths demonstrate those guidelines in actual practice. The two most famous and most highly respected of the Hadith collections are Sahih Bukhari and Sahih Muslim. However, there are other collections that are recognized and respected.

Hadiths are classified as *sahih* (sound), *hassan* (good), and *da'if* (weak), and there are numerous sub-classifications, as well. This is the way the Muslims avoid obeying the different teachings they do not like for the moment. They can always blame it on the translation!

Remember, they can lie for the sake of their religion! And they can change whatever they do not like or that they feel does not apply to them.

# THE QUR'AN

The Qur'an, or the words of Allah, are said to have been revealed to Muhammed in the 7th century A.D. over a span of twenty-two years. The basic tenets of Islam are in the Qur'an.

The Qur'an was compiled in its present form about thirty years after the death of Muhammed. During the lifetime of Muhammed, the Qur'an was written on pieces of stone and other objects.

The Qur'an was revealed in the Arabic language. Muslims learn their prayers in Arabic, which are verses from the Qur'an. The Muslims are to encourage all to learn the language so they can read it in its original form. Although translations have been historically discouraged by Muslim scholars because they are, in effect, interpretations, they do exist in dozen of languages.

# IN THE LAST DAYS

The following are prophecies on the Last Days. The Qur'an was translated only within the last few decades because it has been so closely held by the Muslims. Many people believe, however, that the Muslims knew that when the Qur'an was translated, many people would rise up against it and speak the truth. This, in fact, is exactly what is happening.

Below are some Hadiths about the Muslims' point of view of the Last Days. I am sure you will find this very interesting!

*volume 4, book 56, number 808:*

*Narrated 'Ali:*

*I relate the traditions of Allah's Apostle to you for I would rather fall from the sky than attribute something to him falsely. But when I tell you a thing which is between you and me, then no doubt, war is guile. I heard Allah's Apostle saying, "In the last days of this world there will appear some young foolish people who will use (in their claim) the best speech of all people (i.e. the Qur'an) and they will abandon Islam as an arrow going through the game. Their belief will not go beyond their throats (i.e. they will have practically no belief), so wherever you meet them, kill them, for he who kills them shall get a reward on the Day of Resurrection.*

*Volume 6, Book 61, Number 578:Narrated Abu Said Al-Khudri:*

*I heard Allah's Apostle saying, "There will appear some people among you whose prayer will make you look down upon yours, but they will recite the Qur'an which will not exceed their throats (they will not act on it) and they will go out of Islam as an arrow goes out through the game whereupon the archer would examine the arrowhead but see nothing, and look at the unfeathered arrow but see nothing, and look at the arrow feathers but see nothing, and finally he suspects to find something in the lower part of the arrow."*

# CHANGING YOUR RELIGION

Changing your religion from Islam may be hazardous to your health. In fact, once you have converted to Islam, or rather (reverted) as they would call it, you are forbidden to change. And they say they have the right to kill you.

*Volume 9, Book 84, Number 57:Narrated 'Ikrima:*

**Some Zanadiqa (atheists) were brought to 'Ali and he burnt them. The news of this event, reached Ibn 'Abbas who said, "If I had been in his place, I would not have burnt them, as Allah's Apostle forbade it, saying, 'Do not punish anybody with Allah's punishment (fire).' I would have killed them according to the statement of Allah's Apostle, 'Whoever changed his Islamic religion, then kill him.'"**

*Volume 9, Book 84, Number 58: Narrated Abu Burda:*

**Abu Musa said, "I came to the Prophet along with two men (from the tribe) of Ash'ariyin, one on my right and the other on my left, while Allah's Apostle was brushing his teeth (with a Siwak), and both men asked him for some employment. The Prophet said, 'O Abu Musa (O 'Abdullah bin Qais!).' I said, 'By Him Who sent you with the Truth, these two men did not tell me what was in their hearts and I did not feel (realize) that they were seeking employment.' As if I were**

*looking now at his Siwak being drawn to a corner under his lips, and he said, 'We never (or, we do not) appoint for our affairs anyone who seeks to be employed. But O Abu Musa! (or 'Abdullah bin Qais!) Go to Yemen.'"*

*The Prophet then sent Mu'adh bin Jabal after him and when Mu'adh reached him, he spread out a cushion for him and requested him to get down (and sit on the cushion). Behold: There was a fettered man beside Abu Muisa. Mu'adh asked, "Who is this (man)?" Abu Muisa said, "He was a Jew and became a Muslim and then reverted back to Judaism." Then Abu Muisa requested Mu'adh to sit down but Mu'adh said, "I will not sit down till he has been killed. This is the judgment of Allah and His Apostle (for such cases) and repeated it thrice." Then Abu Musa ordered that the man be killed, and he was killed. Abu Musa added, "Then we discussed the night prayers and one of us said, 'I pray and sleep, and I hope that Allah will reward me for my sleep as well as for my prayers.'"*

# PUNISHMENT OF DISBELIEVERS AT WAR WITH ALLAH AND HIS APOSTLE

*"When you encounter the unbelievers, strike off their heads, until ye have made a great slaughter among them...." (Surah 47:4)*

*"...Make war upon such of those to whom the Scriptures have been given as believe not in Allah, or in the Last Day, and who forbid not what Allah and His Apostle have forbidden...until they pay tribute..." (Surah 9:29).*

*Volume 8, Book 82, Number 794:*

*Narrated Anas:*

*Some people from the tribe of 'Ukl came to the Prophet and embraced Islam. The climate of Medina did not suit them, so the Prophet ordered them to go to the (herd of milch) camels of charity and to drink, their milk and urine (as a medicine). They did so, and after they had recovered from their ailment (became healthy) they turned renegades (reverted from Islam) and killed the shepherd of the camels and took the camels away. The Prophet sent (some people) in their pursuit and so they were (caught and) brought, and the Prophets ordered that their hands and legs should be cut off and that their eyes should be branded with heated pieces of iron, and that their cut hands and legs should not be cauterized, till they die.*

*Volume 8, Book 82, Number 795:Narrated Anas:*

**The Prophet cut off the hands and feet of the men belonging to the tribe of 'Uraina and did not cauterize (their bleeding limbs) till they died.**

# THE MARRIAGE CONTRACT
# AGREEMENT

If you decide you want to go ahead with a Muslim marriage even after you have read this book, we suggest that you at least have an "agreement" signed by the both of you. In case of divorce, this could help some. A wonderful Christian sister of mine, who has been a great support and help to me, thought of this idea. She, too, is married to a Muslim. (Thanks "C," and blessings to you.) May this contract the Lord gave her help many.

Using the contractual elements listed below is a good starting point, but it would be best, and much wiser, to have the final document prepared by an attorney.

Of course, most women do not enter marriage with the expectation that they will be divorced. In fact, I know of a few Muslim/Christian marriages that have lasted over twenty years, but these are rare exceptions. With a well thought-out marriage contract, you can protect yourself—just in case.

While a marriage contract (or pre-nuptial agreement) is an uncommon concept to most of us in the United States and western world, it is expected within the Muslim community. This is standard practice because, in Islam, marriage is a contract; marriages are not based on love and commitment before God. Since marriage is a contract, the parties can agree to put all kinds of clauses in that contract. Basically, any clause that does not contradict Islamic law or the basic purpose of marriage is permitted. Among the specific clauses that historically have been recognized in Islamic law are:

1) The dowry amount (or *mahr*) or gift to the bride, of a financial or property amount given up front at the time of marriage or deferred (in whole or in part) to be paid upon death or in the case of divorce. This is very significant and do not be afraid to ask for a large amount or a house, etc., because this is all she will get in the case of divorce or inheritance. A portion deferred is good because it provides for the expectation that the husband will become more prosperous as he becomes more successful in his business.

2) The marriage will not be polygamous (i.e., husband agrees no wives already exist and that he will not take a second wife).

3) Specification of the wife's financial independence and ownership of property (the parties can also delineate ownership of specific items in case of divorce, such as the home, furniture, etc.);

4) Right of wife to education and/or employment and/or right to travel. She can also stipulate where she will live or not live (e.g., she will only live in the U.S.).

5) Right of wife to initiate divorce proceedings without consent of the husband.

The above mentioned clauses are those things that will be acceptable under Islamic jurisprudence. However, assuming the couple will reside in a non-Muslim country, I would also advise incorporating the following additional clauses:

6) There should be no compulsion, coercion or force

for the wife or children to practice Islam; wife is free to explain and practice her faith with the children;

7) The children will reside in the United States with their mother.

Including children in these contract specifications is important because Islam teaches that the children belong to the father and that they will be Muslim. If a divorce occurs and this has not been stipulated in the contract, it is likely that the courts will award custody to the father simply because the ceremony was an Islamic one. The more you can stipulate in the contract, even if it would not normally be binding under Islamic jurisprudence, the better it will be in the United States court system. These are only suggestions. Be sure to adapt the terms to fit your situation and, by all means, consult with a licensed attorney.

# THE SALVATION OF THE MUSLIMS

It has been said that it takes over one hundred times for someone who was raised Muslim to start hearing the gospel with any sense of belief. It is like saying a harsh word to someone. One harsh word takes over one thousand kind words to replace it.

Sadly, there is only one missionary per one million Muslims. Along with that, 35 percent of the lost/unsaved people in the world are Muslims: Yes, the harvest is white, but the laborers are few.

Our hearts burn deep with the burden for the Muslims. Jesus died for them just as He did for others. It is God's will that *all* be saved and that none should perish. The hearts of those who have joined together in this ministry are also deeply burdened about the abuse of the women and children in any culture.

Zennah Ministries, Inc. stands firm in our belief in the sanctity of the institution of marriage; and more importantly, in the power of Jesus Christ. It is not impossible for a Muslim to be saved. Many Muslims are coming to Christ. We need to show them the love of Christ.

However, women should be advised that converting a Muslim man to Christianity is very difficult and rare. And no one should ever marry with the hopes or thoughts that the other person will change. If you are already married to a Muslim man, you should be faithful in prayer for your mate.

The scriptures in 1 Corinthians 7 and Ephesians 5 explain God's view on marriage and divorce. It is important to remember that God has a plan for each person.

Paul states in 1 Corinthians 7:16: "For how do you know, O wife, whether you will save your husband? Or how do you know, O husband, whether you will save your wife? Nevertheless, each one should retain the place in life that the Lord assigned to him and to which God has called him."

As we mentioned earlier, God hates divorce. However, according to the Bible, grounds for divorce are: If the unbeliever wants to leave, and in the case of adultery.

In the case of abuse, you should seek help, a place of safety or maybe a separation.

Only the Lord can direct you in this area. You must seek Him for direction in your life. Trust God and study His word. Yoke yourself with believers, and never give up. Pray without stopping, holding fast to the Lord and His words. Be confident in this: Prayer does change things.

We at Zennah Ministries, Inc. would like to add that we do not believe all Muslim men abuse their wives, but when a religion teaches and condones that it is OK to do so, you see much more of this.

Abuse is abuse and is wrong in any religion, form or fashion. If you are being abused, we are here to help!

Help stop abuse…It hurts!

God bless!

# WHAT CHRISTIANS SHOULD EXPECT WHEN THEY MARRY

The purpose of this section of the book is to compare and contrast the Christian marriage to the Islamic marriage.

## WHAT IS A CHRISTIAN MARRIAGE?

One of the first false concepts of marriage is that it is designed to make you happy. However, if you marry for that reason, you are setting yourself up for failure.

Yes, marriage is wonderful and it can make you happy, but it also should be something ordained and blessed of God: It should bring and give Him glory.

Before marrying, the Christian man and woman should first ponder these very important questions: How can we together bring God glory? Can we serve the Lord better alone or with a mate? Do we have the same goals, same purposes? Do we have the same visions and the same dreams?

You see, the purpose of marriage is not for our glory, gain, purpose, desires or lust. Instead, a marriage that is ordained by God will be for the gain of His kingdom. "But seek first his kingdom and his righteousness, and all these things will be given to you as well" (Matt. 5:33).

On the other hand, in Islam they have no concept of this at all. Instead, the purpose of marriage is considered to be limited to the fulfillment of the man's desires...and procreation.

A Christian marriage is two becoming one flesh, one man and one woman...working together with the one goal of helping to further the kingdom of God.

In Islam they have no idea of this at all. Marriage is only for the man's benefit. The woman is nothing more than a possession. The Muslim man may have up to four wives at one time and also have concubines. There is no oneness in these marriages at all.

But what does the Word of God say?

> And the LORD God said, *It is* not good that the man should be alone; I will make him an help meet for him.
> —GENESIS 2:18, EMPHASIS ADDED

## GOD'S PURPOSE FOR MARRIAGE

Woman was created to be a loving companion and helper for man. As such, she is to share his responsibility and cooperate with him in fulfilling God's purpose for his life and the life of their family.

Therefore, the husband and wife should view one another as being a gift from God, and not regard each other according to the flesh!

Along with this, marriage partners are called to help one another become the man or woman God wants his or her partner to be!

> And Adam gave names to all cattle, and to the fowl of the air, and to every beast of the field; but for Adam there was not found an help meet for

for Adam there was not found an help meet for him. And the LORD God caused a deep sleep to fall upon Adam, and he slept: and he took one of his ribs, and closed up the flesh instead thereof; And the rib, which the LORD God had taken from man, made he a woman, and brought her unto the man. And Adam said, This *is* now bone of my bones, and flesh of my flesh: she shall be called Woman, because she was taken out of Man. Therefore shall a man leave his father and his mother, and shall cleave unto his wife: and they shall be one flesh.

—GENESIS 2:20-24, KJV, EMPHASIS ADDED

In this passage of the Word of God, we see how God chose to use the rib of Adam—so the man and woman would be side by side. It is important to note that only because of the curse was man placed over the woman. (See Genesis 3:16.)

Conversely, the false prophet of Islam said that because woman was made from the rib of man, women are crooked. According to this false teaching, man would not be able to straighten out the woman and if he tried to do so, the man would break her.

Oftentimes in Islam, instead of the man leaving his father and mother, they will all live together and the new wife must also obey and submit to the mother-in-law. The mother-in-law has rights over the wife of her son, and nothing belongs to the wife. Not only does everything go to the mother-in-law first, but she can also take anything she pleases from the daughter-in-law!

However, the Bible calls for something very different:

According to God's Word, the man is to leave his father and mother (Genesis 2:24). In the beginning, and foremost institution on earth. God's plan for marriage consists of one male and one female who become "One Flesh" (i.e. united physically and spiritually). This instruction excludes adultery, polygamy, homosexuality, immoral living and unscriptural divorce.

(Alone = All in ONE)

We see in Genesis 3:16 that because of the curse, God put man over woman. "Unto the woman he said, I will greatly multiply thy sorrow and thy conception; in sorrow thou shalt bring forth children; and thy desire shall be to thy husband, and he shall rule over thee" (KJV).

## CHOOSING A PARTNER

When seeking a marriage partner, prudence is more important than appearance. God's wisdom, guidance and blessing are essential if we want to have a happy marriage. A believer should seek to marry someone who is deeply committed to the Lord Jesus, His Word and the standards of His kingdom. Marriage to a person of godly character is a special blessing of God.

> Better *is* a dry morsel, and quietness therewith, than an house full of sacrifices *with* strife.
> —PROVERBS 17:1, KJV, EMPHASIS ADDED

> House and riches *are* the inheritance of fathers: and a prudent wife *is* from the LORD.
> —PROVERBS 19:14, KJV, EMPHASIS ADDED

> Whoso findeth a wife findeth a good thing, and obtaineth favour of the LORD.
> —PROVERBS 18:22, KJV

Before we make a covenant with someone, we must be completely sure that this is the person God wants be completely sure that this is the person God wants for us.

As trials come in the marriage, oftentimes it is the assurance you have knowing you've made the right decision that becomes the saving grace in the marriage. Knowing this can really pull you through those tough times.

The story of Rebekah in Genesis 24:12-28 is a wonderful example of God revealing His selection of partners of marriage:

> And he said, O LORD God of my master Abraham, I pray thee, send me good speed this day, and shew kindness unto my master Abraham. Behold, I stand *here* by the well of water; and the daughters of the men of the city come out to draw water: And let it come to pass, that the damsel to whom I shall say, Let down thy pitcher, I pray thee, that I may drink; and she shall say, Drink, and I will give thy camels drink also: *let the same be* she *that* thou hast appointed for thy servant Isaac; and thereby shall I know that thou hast shewed kindness unto my master. And it came to pass, before he had done speaking, that, behold, Rebekah came out, who was born to Bethuel, son of Milcah, the wife of Nahor, Abraham's brother, with her pitcher upon her shoulder. And the damsel *was* very fair to look upon, a virgin, neither had any man known her: and she went down to the well, and filled her pitcher, and came up. And the servant ran to meet her, and said, Let me, I pray thee, drink a little water of thy pitcher. And she said, Drink, my lord: and she hasted, and let down her pitcher upon her hand, and gave him drink. And when

she had done giving him drink, she said, I will draw *water* for thy camels also, until they have done drinking. And she hasted, and emptied her pitcher into the trough, and ran again unto the well to draw *water*, and drew for all his camels. And the man wondering at her held his peace, to wit whether the LORD had made his journey prosperous or not. And it came to pass, as the camels had done drinking, that the man took a golden earring of half a shekel weight, and two bracelets for her hands of ten *shekels* weight of gold; And said, Whose daughter *art* thou? tell me, I pray thee: is there room *in* thy father's house for us to lodge in? And she said unto him, I *am* the daughter of Bethuel the son of Milcah, which she bare unto Nahor. She said moreover unto him, We have both straw and provender enough, and room to lodge in. And the man bowed down his head, and worshipped the LORD. And he said, Blessed *be* the LORD God of my master Abraham, who hath not left destitute my master of his mercy and his truth: I *being* in the way, the LORD led me to the house of my master's brethren. And the damsel ran, and told *them of* her mother's house these things (KJV, EMPHASIS ADDED).

## GOD IS A GOD OF DIVINE ORDER

Although we are all free in Christ, there still is an order of command we all must follow, for even the head of Christ is God the Father.

Now I want you to realize that the head of every man is Christ, and the head of the woman is man, and the head of Christ is God. . . . In the

Lord, however, woman is not independent of man nor is man independent of woman. For as woman came from man, so also man is born of woman. But everything comes from God.

—1 CORINTHIANS 11:3, 11–12

There is neither Jews nor Greek, slave nor free, male nor female, for you are all one in Christ Jesus.

—GALATIANS 3:28

The Book of Ephesians gives very clear examples of the relationship of the husband and wife.

Wives be subject—be submissive and adapt yourselves to your own husbands as (a service) to the Lord. For the husband is head of the wife as Christ is the Head of the church, Himself the Savior of (His) body. As the church is subject to Christ so let wives also be subject in everything to their husbands. Husbands, love your wives, as Christ loved the church and gave Himself up for her. So that He might sanctify her, having cleansed her by the washing of water and the Word, That He might present the church to Himself in glorious splendor, without spot or wrinkle or any such things—That she might be Holy and faultless. Even so husbands should love their wives as (being in a sense) their own bodies. He who loves his own wife loves himself . . . For no man ever hated his own flesh, but nourishes and carefully protects and cherishes it, as Christ does the church. Because we are members (parts) of His body. For this reason a man shall leave his father and mother and shall be joined to his wife, and the two shall become one flesh. This mystery is very great; but I speak concerning (the relation of) Christ and the church. However, let each man of you (without exception) love his wife as (being in a sense) his very own self; and let the wife see that she respects and reverences her husband— that she notices him, regards him, honors him, prefers him, venerates and esteems him; and that she defers to him, praises him, and loves and admires him exceedingly.

—EPHESIANS 5:22–33, AMP

Speak to one another with psalms, hymns and spiritual songs. Sing and make music in your heart to the Lord, always giving thanks to God the Father for everything, in the name of our Lord Jesus Christ. Submit to one another out of reverence of Christ.

—EPHESIANS 5:19–21

## CHARACTER QUALITIES THAT ARE IMPORTANT FOR MARRIAGE TODAY

*What you expect from others should also be evident in your life.* This applies to both husbands and wives. Christian marriage is not one-sided: It is one unit working together!

- Willingness to serve, humility
- Sexual purity
- Devotion to Christ
- Right priorities
- Right beliefs
- Commitment to church
- Loving attitude

- Self-control
- Honesty
- Beauty below the skin
- Responsibility
- Good relationship with parents

Most important is what is said in:

> Do not be yoked together with unbelievers. For what do righteousness and wickedness have in common? Or what fellowship can light have with darkness? What harmony is there between Christ and Belial? What does a believer have in common with an unbeliever?
> —2 CORINTHIANS 6:14–15

In God's eyes, marriage is a covenant, which is the secret that alone ensures the success of the marriage relationship. Once this secret is forgotten or ignored, marriage loses its sanctity and therefore loses strength and stability. A Christian must not go into a marriage covenant with an unbeliever. Second Corinthians 6:14–15 clearly states that Christians should not be yoked together with unbelievers, and compares it to having fellowship with darkness.

So two Christians are to come together on the common ground of Christ. This is essential because they are to become one, and certainly such a union cannot be half light and half dark, functioning with completely different purposes and in opposing spiritual kingdoms. We can further see the importance of this when we examine 1 Corinthians 12:12–31, where Paul describes how that no part of the body can function effectively on its own. Here Paul is speaking of the members of the church, but this concept also applies to fulfillment and wholeness in a marriage relationship is by entering into a committed relationship (covenant) where the husband and wife are functioning together as one, in accordance with God's plan for marriage.

Functioning together as one, in a committed relationship, is essential if the man and his wife are to fulfill the calling of God on their lives, both corporately and individually. We can see in the Book of Malachi how God's anger was kindled when people began to take things into their own hands, thinking they could do things their own way. In Malachi, chapter 2, we read that Israel had come to view marriage as a relationship for which they might set their own standards, including being free to initiate or terminate the union on their own terms. Clearly, a wrong view of marriage was the root cause of this practice.

A wrong view of marriage is also what leads to abuse and bondage of women who marry Muslim men today. The Muslim religion teaches that the husband is the one who gives the permission for the wife to enter into heaven. Supposedly, the wife is judged on how well she obeyed and served her husband rather than on whether or not she had a personal relationship with the Lord.

However, this teaching is far from the truth because God's Word tells us that we will each individually stand before the Lord and give an account to Him alone. Our own works or good deeds will not gain us entrance into heaven. Instead, we will have eternal fellowship in Heaven with the Lord by the grace of God and the cross of Jesus.

Although Christianity and the Muslim religion both teach that a woman should dress in modest attire, the reasons given for this are very different. In Islam, modesty once again goes back to being for the good of the husband. The woman is required to dress modesty as a way of showing respect to her husband and saving her beauty only for him.

Let us look at what the Bible says about this:

## IMPORTANT ELEMENTS IN MARRIAGE

### *Respect: Wives and Husbands*

> Wives, in the same way be submissive to your husbands so that, if any of them do not believe the word, they may be won over without words when they see the behavior of their wives, when they see the purity and reverence of your lives. Your beauty should not come from outward adornment, such as braided hair and the wearing of gold jewelry and fine clothes. Instead, it should be that of your inner self, the unfading beauty of a gentle and quiet spirit, which is of great worth in God's sight. For this is the way the holy women of the past who put their hope in God, used to make themselves beautiful. They were submissive to their own husbands, like Sarah, who obeyed Abraham and called him her master.
>
> — 1 PETER 3:1–6

If we look at 1 Peter 3: 3–4, we can see that gaudy or expensive adornment is contrary to the spirit of modesty that God desires for the Christian wife to have. Instead, what God highly values in a Christian wife is a gentle disposition that seeks to honor Him by giving herself to help her husband and her family achieve

God's will for their lives. This is very different from the Muslim teaching that puts pleasing the husband right at the center of the wife's goals, intentions and purpose for life.

As we further examine verses 3–4, we learn more about the attributes God values in a wife.

The adjective "gentle" describes an unassuming disposition that expresses itself in gracious submissiveness and a concern for others.

The adjective "quiet" refers to a disposition that is not boisterous and does not create disturbances. In other words, God declares that true beauty is a matter of character and not a matter of decoration.

Christians wives must be loyal to Christ and His Word in a world governed by materialism, manipulative fashion, self-assertion, obsession with sex and contempt for the values of home and family.

Christians are told to only marry those with like faith.

Unlike Christians, the Muslim man may marry a Christian or Jewish woman for the benefit of her conversion to the Muslim religion.

While in Malachi 2:16, the Lord God says that He hates divorce, God's Word does tell us that there are reasons for divorce: Two that are very clear are adultery and if the unbeliever wants to leave.

However, in Islam, only the husband can divorce the wife. The reason can be for anything the husband doesn't like about her. The wife, on the other hand, cannot divorce the husband.

We must remember that God put the very first marriage together, that of Adam and Eve. Also in reference to marriage, Jesus said in Matthew 19:6, "So they are no longer two, but one. Therefore what God has joined together, let not man separate."

As pointed out earlier, Islam does not see marriage

as two becoming one flesh that is not to be separated.

Of course, if you are not in relationship with God and His Son Jesus, then how can He put the right mate into your life? First things first—You must first be reconciled to God through His Son, Jesus Christ. Then, and only then, will you be able to enjoy marriage according to God's perfect plan.

MARRIED TO
MUHAMMED
MARRIED TO
MUHAMMED
MARRIED TO

# PART 3

# ARE YOU BEING ABUSED?

### *P.A.T.H.S. Information about Abuse*

If you are being abused, you are not alone. It is common for an abused woman to think she is the only one this is happening to, yet in Canada, one in every four women is, or has been, abused by an intimate partner—a man she lives with or has lived with. Also, you are not to blame. No matter what your partner or others have said, you are not responsible for the abuse. All of us have faults and all of us have disagreements within a relationship. However, this doesn't mean that we deserve to be abused. Your partner is the one choosing to be violent—he is responsible, not you.

You cannot make the abuse stop by changing your behavior. In fact, abusive behavior often becomes more severe and more frequent over time. No matter how accommodating you are, the abusive behavior won't stop until the abuser decides to change. Meanwhile, you need to get legal information and find a safe place to live. There are people who want to help you, people who work in shelters and other agencies.

They've been trained to provide information, support and counseling. Their help could make a profound difference to your life.

By abuse, we mean sexual, physical, emotional, financial abuse—conduct labeled domestic violence, family violence, spousal assault, dating violence, battering.

Abuse is when someone who is supposed to care about you threatens your health, your well-being or your financial situation. You don't deserve to be treated that way. And you can't change the abuser. Only the abuser can do that. But you can ask for help and get information. There are people who care and are ready to listen. Talk to someone you trust—a friend, family member, doctor, nurse, social worker or the police.

The societal issue of battered women has been labeled as wife abuse, spousal abuse, and conjugal, domestic or family violence. For the purposes of this manual we will use the term battered or abused women, which refers specifically to assaultive or abusive behavior committed by a man against a woman with whom he has an intimate, sexual, usually co-habitating, relationship. (The definition is sex specific because while *men* may also be victims of battering, the numbers are very small. The abuse usually isn't accompanied by the threat of physical abuse, and the power balance is distinctly different. Abuse of men in our society is not reinforced by the social, religious and economic factors that are operative in women's experience.) Battering can take many forms including, but not limited to:

*Physical Abuse:* may include, but is not limited to: pushing, slapping, punching, choking, kicking and breaking bones; throwing objects; abandoning her in an unsafe place; deprivation of food, water, clothing;

confining her in a closet, room or building; locking her out of her home; using weapons against her; murder.

*Sexual Abuse:* may include, but not limited to: forced, coerced or unwanted touching or sex with partner; withholding of sex or affection; demanding that she wear more/less provocative clothing; forced sex with objects, friends, animals, or other sexual practices that make her feel humiliated or degraded; insisting that she act out pornographic fantasies; denial of her sexuality, sexual feelings or desirability as a sexual partner; rape.

*Emotional Abuse:* may include, but is not limited to: withdrawal of affection; jealousy; denial of her right to feelings or emotions; putdowns, constant criticism; name calling; isolating her from friends and family; controlling her activities; denying her any personal pleasures or outside interests; destruction of property, pets or treasured objects; threats to harm friends or family; forcing her to watch her children being abused without being allowed to intervene; making her account for every minute, every action; controlling her with fear, threats of suicide, threats on her life.

*Economic Abuse:* may include, but is not limited to: allowing a woman to have no money of her own, no money for emergencies, not even her own earnings; forcing her to account for and justify all money spent; not allowing her to earn money or improve her earning capacity.

*Spiritual Abuse:* may include, but is not limited to: breaking down one's belief system (cultural or religious); being punished or ridiculed for one's beliefs; preventing the practice of beliefs.

# LETTERS FROM THE
# DEAR W. L. CATI COLUMN

Dear W. L. Cati;

I went to two years of counseling, but my therapist really didn't understand my situation as well as the counselor that led this support group. My therapist encouraged me to be dependent on her. Whereas, the support group counselor helped me to see my strengths. One thing that I found very helpful was when my support counselor told us how we become our own worst enemy parroting the verbal abuse our husbands dish out even when he's not around, so when he comes home it just reinforces what we've been saying to ourselves all day. I'm so stupid...,I'm so ugly..., I'm so fat..., I'm .... She told us to change all those statements to the positive, but she understood that for most of us, we were so worn down with trying to please and do the right thing that we didn't have the energy to turn a negative self statement into a positive one, so she said that for now we should wear a rubber band around our wrist and whenever we started saying something negative to ourselves we should flick the rubber band and say, "Stop it," out loud, if possible and silently if that was all we could do. Although that sounds very corny, I found it very helpful to start build up my self-esteem so that I could endure his attacks and know that they were not true. He was dealing with his own frustrations at work and it actually had nothing to do with me. I just was a safe outlet.

I knew I was really parroting what my husband was saying when I made a wrong turn while driving my two year old somewhere. I said, "I'm so stupid.." and she said, "Mommy are you being stupid AGAIN!?!" That's when it hit me that I really needed to make a change. After a particularly brutal attack from my husband, I still went to Turkey with him. I can tell you that the abuse got much worse in Turkey. Before he was afraid to hit me anywhere where I'd bruise, but in Turkey he was unrepentant and didn't care where he hit me. We turned down social invitations because I was not well (I had a hand print shaped bruise on my face and a black eye and a swollen lip.) I was socially isolated because he didn't want any one to see me like that, but he always let me know that it was my own fault that he was driven to abuse me. I think "C's" suggestion to just not be around when he's ready to leave is a good one. I think in my situation I would have been afraid not to be there. . . but it's good advice all the same. If he had gone by himself, I would have had a summer of peace. I don't know if this helps, but my divorce paper says that it was he who deserted our marriage by abusing me, even though it was I who filed for divorce. I had felt very guilty about filing for divorce. The whole proceedings took about two years. I had no idea the Court would say that it was he who deserted the marriage. His wife beating issue is just another attempt by Muslim apologists to white wash Islam in the West. The following come from their Hadith and it amazes me that modern scholars are trying to alter the meaning of these and getting away with it. Maybe the staunch Muslim scholars don't mind as long as it brings in converts ... sorta like the ol' bait-and-switch sales pitch. ***Beating Your Wife... The Prophet (SAW) said: "When one of you inflicts a beating, he should avoid striking the face." (Narrated Abu Huraira)*** The man according to the Qur'an has the responsibility to admonish his wife, and the right to desert her sexually, and to beat her to correct any rebelliousness in her behavior.

***The translator of Mishkrat Al_Massabih wrote in a footnote of Fatwa by Qazi Khan that said beating the wife mildly is "allowed in four cases (1) When she wears fineries though wanted by the husband, (2) When she is called for sexual intercourse and she refuses and she refuses without any lawful excuse, (3) When she is ordered to take a bath (to clean herself) from impurities for prayer and she refuses and (4) When she goes abroad without permission of her husband." (60)***

In another footnote the translator of Mishkat Al-Masabih said, ***"No wife shall refuse her husband what he wants from her except on religious grounds ie. at the time of menstrual flow or fasting. Some theologians regard the refusal as unlawful as the husband may get enjoyment from his wife in other ways, by embracing, kissing, etc. The duty of the wife*** *is to give him comforts in his bed whenever he wants her," (61)* (emphasis added) This beating is the husband's unquestionable right.

Ibn Kathir in his commentary mentioned a Hadith on the authority of zal Ash'ath Ibn as-Qays who was visiting Omar and at the time. "Omar took his wife and beat her, then said to Ash'arth: Memorize three things from me.

Which I memorized from the prophet who said: "The man is not to be asked why he beat his wife....."(62)

Dear W. L. Cati

My hands are trembling. I thought I would never begin a post like this again but this is what happened. This morning M. asked my little guy if I ever took him in meetings. My kid said yes and hell broke loose.

He threw things at me, call me all sorts of names, spit at me, etc. I called the police, not to arrest him but to let him know the definition of abuse and that I won't take it.

This had a tremendous affect on him. Payback is still in progress. I lost many things. I need your help. Now, he will watch me a lot closer. I can't take em to the meetings.

Please send me some narrative stories on Christian principals that I could tell my kids. I am not squared away with my own knowledge, and now I have to teach em.

I am going to social services this Monday with the report. please pray for me. As of now, Mo. is in shock since that is one of the worse things I could of done (in his culture). The police kept asking me why don't I work, I wanted to explain to them that last time I worked he had big plans of travel to Egypt and Islamic school. But I couldn't. Men stick together. M. convinced the police that I was an hysterical female, and they left making jokes with him.

My second daughter stuck with her father telling the police that she hates me. And when I asked her if what she saw as my treatment was alright she said that I deserved it, that I should be a Muslim.

I would like to know if God loves some people more than others. He fashioned me, and I am his creation. He is love. but I wish he would love me more.

Does anyone know why he didn't love the Jews of Germany during Hitler more?

I know how this sounds, I hope that God forgives me for being presumptuous when I should remember all my many sins of the past and any love is undeserved, but I want him to love me more. By the way I asked this before and they said that I had surprised them at how long I have studied and how do I have the nerve to think this.

Dear W. L. Cati,

I have been divorced for about 10 years. I was married to a Turk. I met him when I was on vacation in Turkey. We have two children. My son is now 11 and my daughter will be 13 on Thursday. V was abusive and our marriage deteriorated. He dated a couple women after getting divorced from me (before also I'm told—but that's another story). He was used to having a woman take care of him (his mother), so when his last girl friend broke up with him, he completely lost it mentally. She broke up with him because he was not Catholic—after two years of dating. He went back to Turkey a year ago February. He expects to come back. I'm probably one of his only friends in this world. He calls about once a month "to check on the kids," but only talks to me. He believes he is the reincarnation of Christ. This is giving him the power he wanted— he is now the most powerful person on earth. He doesn't have to listen to anyone, since he is god and he will never work another day in his life. (His poor mother!)

I'm on very good terms with his mother. My daughter spent the summer with her, summer before last. She always wanted a daughter — she had two boys. When I fell in love with V, I also fell in love with Turkey, the language, the culture, the history. It was thrilling to stand in the very stadium where Paul spoke to the Ephesians. It was exciting to see the bible stories come alive. I was intrigued to investigate a different social order than the one I'm used to.

Dear W. L. Cati,
I read your posting on the Internet.
I am W, a convert to Christianity from Islam. I used to be a muslim husband to an American woman from a jewish background. After her conversion to Islam she had to follow my strict ways. I was abusive both physically and emotionally, I could never see how bad I was until I looked at islam from the outside. My mother who is a Christian is still married to my muslim father. I have seen it all. I just wanted to jot this line to encourage you to keep on fighting the battle.

W

Dear W. L. Cati,

I just finished reading your testimony on the Internet and enjoyed it very much. I accepted Jesus Christ as my Savior in 1983.

All my life I dreamed of marrying that special someone. When I became a Christian, I began to ask the Lord [to] send him to me.

Over the next dozen years, I had a number of negative experiences with "Christian" men. One man I dated turned out to be homosexual. Another told me I was demon-possessed and needed an exorcism. Still another was a licensed minister, but spent all of our time together trying to get me into bed.

It was this relationship I was recovering from when I went to Israel and Jordan March of 1996. I met F in a small Muslin village. He was handsome, charming and attentive. Though I knew he was a Muslim, and the Bible forbids marriage between Christians and unbelievers, I wanted to marry him, so I did.

In the beginning, we lived in Jordan with his family. They were very poor. I had some money saved and gave it to them. Life there was very depressing. I couldn't afford to have my car shipped over from the States, and there was nothing to do at home. F left his job in the army because he hated it and made very little money. I was miserable and started to lash out at him.

F applied for a US visa and was refused. it took another year before he was granted one. That was the hardest year of my life. Many times I thought about returning to the States alone. I didn't have any money left, but I could charge my plane ticket to my Visa card and I had friends I could stay with until I got a job.

I drove everyone crazy with my indecision. Then, just when I thought I couldn't take any more, F's visa came through. We flew to the States. F is now in the restaurant business and doing well.

When we were first married, F showed interest in learning about Jesus. I put him in touch with a Baptist missionary who gave him weekly Bible lessons. But after some months F told me he didn't understand Christianity and wanted to return to Islam.

F is now a nominal Muslim, but I believe that could change at any time. I still believe in Jesus although I don't go to church.

Thank you for your testimony; it's very encouraging.

L

Dear L,

It is very sad that our Christian brothers do not live as they should and become the men that the Lord would have them become. I do know that there are many who do follow Christ. My father is one of them. I pray that your husband will find Jesus. He appears to have more of an open heart than most Muslims. I also, pray that you will not experience what I have gone through. If we can be of any help to you, we are here for you.

GOD BLESS,
W. L. CATI

Dear W. L. Cati,

My name is T.P. and I have read your testimony and you have no idea of how much strength I was able to draw from your testimony. I know that it to had to have been God and him alone to take you through the course of events that you described in your testimony. I too am a Christian and have met this very nice man who is Muslim. I know that the first instinct is to run fast in the opposite direction but in this instance the reaction was slightly different. He has such a sweet and gentle spirit about him that is such an attraction to me. I've tried to gather a lot of information on his religion to get a better understanding of the Muslim's way of lie. He's Sunnite Muslim and is very dedicated to what he believes. He knows that I am a Christian yet he never tries to force his religion upon me but should I have a question he will answer it to the best of his ability and if he doesn't know the answer he will find out. I wouldn't say that I'm considering the Muslim way of life but I would say that it has sparked some curiosity. I was brought up in a Christian household and tend to justify my thoughts about any other religion as wanting to be informed and not discrediting someone else just because of the differences in religion. I have experienced a great deal of hurt and disappointments lately so a part of me believes that I could just be at a vulnerable state (which I know is only a trick of the devil). I would like to think that I'm a strong young woman but here lately I tend to doubt so many things and my strength is one. I would like to know something that I didn't get from the end of your testimony, and that is, Did you accept Jesus as your personal Lord and Savior and stay married to Mohammed? If not, how did you deal with that? If so, did the two of you remain married?

My family was introduced to my new friend however, I neglected to tell them that he was a Muslim. I didn't want him to be judged solely on the choice of his decision but for the man he is. As much as I love my family and my fellow Christians I'm aware of the fact that we have a tendency sometimes to be very judgmental and I didn't want to be plagued with that type of stigma just meeting my family for the first time. From one woman to another please invoke upon me some good sound wisdom.

Thank you in advance. I hope to hear from you soon.

SIGNED, TP

Dear TP,

Thank you for your letter. May Jesus bless your openness to know the truth.

To answer your question, Yes.... I came back to Jesus and found my life in Him. Plus, my children have all been saved and are witnesses for the Lord. As far as my husband, no, he didn't come to the Lord. His heart is very hard. When my children and I made our stand for Jesus he kicked us out of the house. It should have been hard, but Jesus is so wonderful, and he is providing all our needs according to His riches in glory.

I have so much to share with you. I just pray that you are ready for truth, sometimes love is blind. I know in my case it was. I wouldn't believe all the stories people would tell me because I said the same thing as you have in your letter.

I have just finished a book called "What to Expect When You Marry a Muslin Man." I would love to send you a copy of it. It is not a pretty story. The book covers everything that you would need to know from knowing your pursuer to divorce.

*For example: Beating Your Wife... The Prophet (SAW) said: "When one of you inflicts a beating, he should avoid striking the face."* (Narrated Abu Huraira)

The man according to the Qur'an has the responsibility to admonish his wife, and the right to desert her sexually, and to beat her to correct any rebelliousness in her behavior.

*The translator of Mishkrat Al_Massabih wrote in a footnote of Fatwa by Qazi Khan that said beating the wife mildly is "allowed in four cases (1) When she wears fineries though wanted by the husband, (2) When she is called for sexual intercourse and she refuses and she refuses without any lawful excuse, (3) When she is ordered to take a bath (to clean herself) from impurities for prayer and she refuses and (4) When she goes abroad without permission of her husband." (60)*

In another footnote the translator of Mishkat Al-Masabih said,

*"No wife shall refuse her husband what he wants from her except on religious grounds ie. at the time of menstrual flow or fasting. Some theologians regard the refusal as unlawful as the husband may get enjoyment from his wife in other ways, by embracing, kissing, etc. The duty of the wife is to give him comforts in his bed whenever he wants her,"* (61) (emphasis added). This beating is the husband's unquestionable right.

Ibn Kathir in his commentary mentioned a

Hadith on the authority of zal Ash'ath Ibn as-Qays who was visiting Omar and at the time. "Omar took his wife and beat her, then said to Ash'arth: Memorize three things from me. Which I memorized from the prophet who said: "The man is not to be asked why he beat his wife....."(62)

This is just one little issue. My ex-husband told me this was not true before we were married. But afterwards, he beat me up I don't know how many times.

PLEASE KEEP IN TOUCH,

MAY JESUS BLESS YOU

Dear W. L. Cati,

i am an american muslim. i married a muslim. from now till the day i die i will be a muslim. it has brought me nothing but peace, love, understanding, compassion and a wonderful husband and father for my children. i used to be a christian. my grandmother was devoted to jesus christ. i went to church three times a week. every time i questioned there were no direct answers from my grandmother or our minister. i must forwarn you do assume you know what islam is until you have lived it. it's a complete way of life. i have seen christian children grow up to hate their mother and father, and show nothing but disrespect to their elders. But i have never seen a muslim man or woman for that matter disobey or disrespect their parents or elder brother and sisters. Everyone sins and has come short of the glory of God, that is between the individual and God. God is the only Judge. Remember this. the bible has many different versions the koran only one. Ask yourself why? Nation of Islam is not true Islamic faith so if this is your proof this is no proof. May God bless you. Ah

Dear Ah:

Please read my testimony. I was a Muslim for almost 7 years, married to a Muslim for 14 years and I have been to Syria four times and Egypt. I am not nor ever have been a part of the Nation of Islam. I have seen many things in the past 14 years. I and my children, plus many women that I talk with on a daily basis, have been subject to Islamic abuse, in all forms possible. I thought it all to be right for many years because of the teachings of Mohammed. One day, I got hit one too many times. I started praying God please show me truth, nothing but truth.

I am not someone out there speaking against something I know nothing about. I lived, walked, believed it, to the point I covered, prayed in Arabic five times a day, and fasted Ramadan. And I was a lot like you. I even brought others to Islam. Please, read this....My Testimony! Found under Answering/Islam.

I know it is long, but as God Almighty is my witness it is the truth. I will be praying for God to show you truth. Jesus is the Way the Truth and the light. No comes to the Father except by HIM. He did die for you, and He loves you so much. I am so sorry you did not get the answers you needed, but ask again. I will pray for you until God gives me the answers you need.

Jesus is Lord,
W. L. Cati

Dear W. L. Cati,
Shame on you so called followers o christ. If

jesus come back today and see you getting wordly gain by selling dirty doctrin, he would tell you that you have nothing to do with the that he convey long time ago.i will invite you in the name of allah to study one true way of life which is islam, so you can by his mersy go to heaven. If you resist the evil of this life, and choose goodness and love you should know the door is always open.

Dear No Name,

Not giving your name shows me that you are not sure of what you believe. I must agree with you on one point: to have worldly gain for the wrong reasons. God does supply all our needs and for those who are in full time service to Him they need money to further His work. As far as studying Islam ... I was a Muslim for many years. I know as much if not more than the average Muslim. I feel that if you really knew about your own religion you would choose another one. I pray that the Lord Jesus will show you the truth.

GOD BLESS YOU,

W. L. CATI

Dear W. L. Cati,

[My husband] was abusive from almost the first day of our marriage and continued we were separated. He was really upset that I did not call off our wedding since I was on my period. This really upset him. What was I going to do, tell everyone that the party was off when they had been cooking for days. He really married me for his green card, no matter what he says. It surprises me that more women convert to islam than men! I wonder if they really read what islam says about women if they would change their minds about converting! Some of the things about the evil eye that I was told also really blew my mind!

I would like to help you with your ministry any way that I can. I would like to start a safe house here but I would have to pray that the Lord would give me the proper location and staffing. I keep trying with the Lord's help to forgive the people that hurt and slandered me and it is hard at times. I also am praying that the Lord will send me the right husband, the one that he has picked out for me! Pray for me in this respect. I will not rush into marriage like my first one.

LOVE, M

Dear M,

God bless you. The truth sets us free. I am so glad that you are out of it all and that Jesus is your Lord. I will pray that He gives the desires of your heart. Seek ye first the Kingdom of God and all these other things will be added to you.

GOD BLESS,
W. L. CATI

Dear Sister W. L. Cati,

I would like to learn more about your ministry to women who were once married to Muslim Men. This is a very important ministry and I would like to be able to recommend you to others that I contact.

GOD BLESS YOU
JIM S

Dear W. L. Cati,

I to am an American woman who was married to a Muhammed, I convert to Islam and wore hijab and tried my utmost to please him and his family. I can relate to so many things in your story . . . worshipping your husband, trying to be a good Muslim. I saw nothing but confusion and hatred in my husband's family also. There truly is no peace in Islam. I just recently became a Christian (I was raised in a fundamentalist home, that kind of a warped view of Christianity). Anyhow, I am probably rambling and not making sense, but if you want to hear my story or just talk to a sister who has been there, email me. My name is J.

Dear J:

God bless you. Your story sounds like many that I read on a daily basis. Believe me you are not alone.

I am in the middle of a divorce also. It has been dragging out now for several months.

We have a ministry here for women that have been dating, married or however involved with a Muslim. It is really growing very fast. God is blessing the work we are doing.

How can we help you?

Love Ya,
W. L. Cati

Dear Ms. Cati,

I read your testimony on that website called Answering Islam. I pretty much passed up the testimonies of people "born" muslim and looked for testimonies of converts like I was.

I would love to ask you to pray for me, I will

do the same for you. Tell me more about your ministry, it sounds really interesting. There is a definite need for it.

Looking forward to hearing more.

Dear W. L. Cati,

I was given your pamphlet by a friend. I hope you and your children are all right. You're in the prayers of many. I am married to a Shiite Muslim man and when I read your story it sounded so familiar in too many ways. I think I married him because of his family, they are so close and that's something I didn't have as a child. A was backslidden when A met and then married him. We've been together more than 17 years and have 3 children. He is not a practicing Muslim but since we've moved amongst his relatives, he has become very adamant about not having anything to do with the religious upbringing of our children. I have a bible study, i.e., "coffee morning with friends," and read my bible in secret. I have all my "Materials" hidden. (I came back to the Lord after a series of crisis with my husband, including womanizing, cocaine addiction, being arrested for sale, possessions of etc.) The story is too long for now. Please let me hear from you if you are able. Yours in Christ, Blue

Dear Blue,

Thank you for your prayers. We are all doing great. The Lord Jesus, is taking care of us. I am so thankful that you came back to the Lord. And even more that you never converted. I too, know what its like to hide my Bible and the associated problems with the children. What is so sad that people do not have a clue what is going on here in the US.

GOD BLESS YOU,<br>W. L. CATI

Dear W. L. Cati;

I just finished reading an article in *Charisma* magazine about women who marry Muslims. I am 19 and a student in Master's Commission. You may have heard about Master's Commission—it is like a Bible college, mainly it is a place where you can find a closer walk with the Lord, and gain ministry experience, and also receive ministry credentials with the AG through Berean courses. This is my second year, and the reason I am writing you is to tell you that: Last summer, I went on my first missions trip. We went to Spain to pass out literature and Bibles and Jesus videos on the southern tip, at the ports where many North Africans are passing through to go home from Europe. We traveled into Morocco twice during my two week trip, once safely and the other getting detained by the police for bringing in Bibles and such. We were kept safe, Praise God!

While I was in Morocco, God laid a burden on my heart first for the people of Morocco, then for Muslims as a whole. My heart is broken for these people, and every time I think about it, I cry. I want to do anything I can to reach them. Anyway, when I first came to Master's Commission almost two years ago, I didn't have any clue of what I wanted to do with my life. I just wanted to find God's perfect plan for my life. I began to seek Him as never before. I was raised in the church, and have called myself a Christian all my life, but never had the real relationship with Him that I should have. In Master's my first year, I was known as the hugger of the bunch. I just love to hold a hurting woman, and love her. We travel and do church services everywhere, and my favorite part was the altar time, when I would get to pray for young girls, and hold them in my arms as they cried. It was "My time!" I loved it! And my director, J, told me at the beginning of that year and many times since, that I am going to disciple. I want more than anything to be married and have a family! I actually was engaged, and broke it off about four months ago, because, although he was called into the ministry, he was not burdened for Muslims the same way that I was. God is calling me in a different direction, and I want to answer His call!

I have thought about being a missionary, but that isn't where my heart is, not overseas. I just told my pastor, G. H., that what I would love to do would be to disciple women who have gotten saved but where once Muslims. And I had no idea that your ministry even existed until I read that article! I don't have any degree to offer or anything, but I have been researching Islam from a Christian standpoint. (I am reading Islam Revealed right now.) I have been encouraged to take a two month MAPS trip overseas, but I was just wondering if you could write me back and tell me if you ever take volunteers or interns or anything. I would love to visit and just see what your ministry is like, and how it functions, and be of any help that I can. I really feel that this area of ministry is where God is leading me. It is 4:20 in the morning and I have to get up at 9:00 for church, so I better go. Thank you for your help and thank you for your ministry. I think it is just awesome what you are doing! May God bless you!

SINCERELY,

A Z

Dear W L Cati,

For 2 years I fighted in court for my children's custody. I had to deliver many medical certificates to prove that I am not insane, because, like I told you I was in a psychiatric clinic for a deep depression. They interviewed the kids and all 5 said that they would never want to live with their mother who was not muslim any more. So the court decided that it was better for the kids to stay in the cultural context where they used to live with their father. Nevertheless, I got the right for a visit of 2 weekends / month and half of the vacations. When my kids refused to visit me on the week-ends, I contacted the guardianship authorities, where they told me that I could make a new process at the guardianship court v/ my ex-husband, in order to oblige him to let the kids visit me and if he still refuses, he would get a penalty or go to jail for some days. That was all. This wouldn't change nothing for my kids, they just would have more grievance against me for having done this to their father. All I can say is, be attentive for your kids. Don't let anybody remove you from their heart in telling them that it is Allah who demands it, because you aren't a "Believer" any more.

GOD BLESS YOU.

D

# W. L. CATI

*AUTHOR, COUNSELOR, CONSULTANT.*
*ORDAINED MINISTER, FORMER BEAUTY*
*QUEEN*

Zennah Ministries, Inc. was founded by W. L. Cati, an American woman who married a Muslim man. Like many other women, she unknowingly converted to Islam at her Arabic wedding ceremony. To go to church, read her Bible or worship Jesus was made very difficult for her. She gave up her faith and fully converted to her husband's Islamic religion. She wore the veil of Islam, and studied the Qur'an. She and her children lived under Muslim control for over fourteen years.

Ms. Cati found Jesus again at the cost of her marriage and luxurious lifestyle. It was a very difficult time for Ms. Cati and her children. With a lot of prayer and faith, they are fully restored back into the body of Christ.

Women all over the world are falling into the Islamic trap. The teachings of the Qur'an condone Muslim men to beat, cheat on, use and even kill their wives if they believe it is necessary. This is a very dangerous religion, yet it is one of the fastest growing religions today.

Zennah Ministries, Inc. reaches out to women who have been unable or too afraid to break out of Islam. With her first-hand knowledge of the Qur'an and her experiences in the Middle East, W. L. Cati shares invaluable advice to women who are involved with a Muslim man.

Cati's experience living among the Arab Muslims has given her a real understanding and unique insight on how to reach out to the Muslims sharing Christ's love.

Cati has been blessed with the favor of Esther, and the anointing of Deborah is on her life. She is seeing many come to know the Lord Jesus.

W. L. Cati has appeared on Christian television and radio. Her life story has been featured in national Christian magazines.

Do you want to hear God's call on your life? "Go out into all the world and preach the gospel."

The harvest is ripe, and the workers are few. Make your life count for Jesus, and reach out to those who are lost!

Ms. Cati is an ordained minister and is available to speak to your church or organization.

Ms. Cati is also available to share her testimony and her singing ministry. She teaches a seminar entitled "Everything You Ever Wanted to Know About Islam, But Didn't Know Who to Ask."

## SEMINAR TOPICS

- *The Different Veils of Islam*
- *Learn how to recognize the culture, tradition, region and religious depth from the veil*
- *Will the real prophet stand up! (Jesus vs. Muhammed)*
- *Learn how to recognize a false prophet and false teaching*
- *Is Allah God?*

- *What do Muslims really believe?*
- *Discover the role of Islam in the Last Days and its impact on everyone in today's world!*

Remember: All things are subject to change; all but God, who never changes!

Zennah Ministries, Inc. has tapes available, information packets and tracts to help you witness to the Muslims. Contact us at the address below.

## MISSION STATEMENT

Zennah Ministries, Inc. is a Christian organization founded to minister to women who are influenced by Muslims. We help to deal with the multitude of tensions and stress brought into the marriage and family by diverse religious and cultural backgrounds; to educate the public through seminars, newsletters, audio and video tapes, preaching, teaching, and other forms of communication, the truth of the Gospel of Jesus Christ, and the differences between the Christian faith and the Muslim religion. Zennah Ministries, Inc. will propagate the faith of the Lord Jesus Christ through evangelism, and desires to establish safe houses and healing houses for those abused. We would love to hear from you!

Zennah Ministries, Inc.
P.O. Box 1235
Holmes Beach, FL 34218
E-Mail: WLCati @aol.com
or
Zennahministries@aol.com
Web Address: http://www.zennahministries.org

Please prayerfully consider helping us to reach out to hurting women, and help us build safe and healing houses all over this country!

Zennah Ministries, Inc. Is a non-profit organization. Your donation is tax deductible! Make any checks payable to: Zennah Ministries, Inc.

Thank you in advance for your giving!

## OUR MINISTRY MANDATES

EVANGELISM—Jesus calls all of us to "go out into the world and preach the good news to all creation" (Mark 16:15). We are sharing hope, faith and the love of Christ with Muslims everywhere. Our materials are now in Africa, Canada, India, the Netherlands, numerous prisons and all across the U.S.

MINISTERING—Jesus tells us that "the Spirit of the Lord is on me, because he has anointed me to preach good news to the poor. He has sent me to proclaim freedom for the prisoners and recovery of sight for the blind, to release the oppressed, to proclaim the year of the Lord's favor" (Luke 4:18, 19). We are reaching out to those that have been affected by the abuse of Islam. We are striving to open safe/healing houses for those oppressed, so they will have a place of refuge—a place where these women can come and grow strong in the admonition of the Lord.

UPHOLDING THE GOSPEL (APOLOGETICS)—Paul teaches us to defend our faith. (See Galatians 1:8.) We are accomplishing this through various forms of communication: training seminars, public speaking, our website, e-mail correspondence, publication of books, pamphlets and tapes. We are committed to enlightening the body of Christ. We say "WAKE UP" to the Church, and heed what the Spirit of the Lord is proclaiming!

# SOURCES, REFERENCES AND CREDITS

Below are some wonderful sources to check into:

"Loving a Muslim" http://www.domini.org/lam/lam.html. A Support Group for Christian Women Dating or Married to Muslims!

"Answering/Islam." (This site can answer many of your questions about Islam.) http://www.answering-islam.org

"Muslim/Christian Dialog Resource Center" http://answering-islam.org/resources/index.html

"The Christian Witness to the Muslim" http://www.biblicalchristianity.freeserve.co.uk/

"The Good Way" http://www.the-good-way.com/

## REFERENCES:

"A Perfect Qur'an" http://www.callnetuk.com/home/aperfectquran/

"A Shi'ite Encyclopedia" Chapter 6.a: Version 2.0 October 1995 http://www.al-islam.org/encyclopedia/chapter6a/ (This is an Islamic web site: They have many articles that may interest you.)

http://www.islam.com/challenges/.

"Striving to Please the Husband by Every Possible means." by Abu Hurariah

"She Should Not Spend Any of His Wealth or Her

Wealth Except With His permission." by Abdullah ibn'
Amr ibn al-'As

Hasan reported by Abu Dawud an Nass'ee and
Ahmad

"She Should Not Permit Anyone to Enter Her
Husband's House Except With His Permission." by Abu
Hurairah

Sahih reported by Al-Haadim and others

"Being A Muslim's Wife" by Abdullah Al Araby

Jamharah Khutah al'Arab 1/145 by Ibn Abbass

"Punishment of Disbelievers at War with Allah and
His Apostle"

"Heaven is for the Man in Islam"

"The X-Rated Paradise of Islam" by Abu Nuwas

"The Place in Pure Islam" by M. Rafiqul-Haqq and P.
Newton

*Compton's Study Bible* King James version on CD

*The Full Life Study Bible*

Kay Campora, *The Wedding Challenge*

Resources for Biblical Communication, "What is the
Promise of Marriage?"

Liberty S. Savard, *Shattering Your Strongholds,
Freedom From Your Struggles*

"About Abuse" http://www.hotpeachpages.org/
paths/medbook/2.html P.A.T.H.S.